American Folksongs
35 Arrangements for Voice & Piano

High Voice

Concert Arrangements by Bryan Stanley & Richard Walters

Cover painting: Winslow Homer, *Boys in a Pasture*, 1874

ISBN 978-0-634-04761-9

Visit Hal Leonard Online at
www.halleonard.com

Contact us:
Hal Leonard
7777 West Bluemound Road
Milwaukee, WI 53213
Email: info@halleonard.com

In Europe, contact:
Hal Leonard Europe Limited
42 Wigmore Street
Marylebone, London, W1U 2RN
Email: info@halleonardeurope.com

In Australia, contact:
Hal Leonard Australia Pty. Ltd.
4 Lentara Court
Cheltenham, Victoria, 3192 Australia
Email: info@halleonard.com.au

Contents

Songs Indexed by Gender

Songs for Either Women or Men

Preface

The folksongs of any culture are a reflection of its passions, humor, values, ideals, struggles, tragedies, extraordinary events and legendary characters. The depth of expression in the songs goes beyond mere entertainment, largely representing the casually epic parade of individual stories of ordinary men and women, representing the nameless millions who are not found in history books.

Surely, many folksongs were written about a specific person whose personal story caught the attention of a minstrel tunesmith, or the songs might be autobiographical. It is reasonable to speculate that some songs are at least partial ficiton, but even those are probably about a generalized, possible or familiar mythical person. Folksongs can make intimate revelations about the thoughts and tastes of those who sang them and listened to them. The fact that these folksongs by unknown writers even survived and became known in an age before broadcasts or recordings is remarkable to a modern sensibility. Most of these songs were not printed in any form until many decades, even centuries, after they first emerged. The only life they had was in the collective memory of a long line of singers, each learning a song only from hearing it sung. Some of the subsequent singers probably fiddled with a song, making it their own in some way, part of a natural sort of mutation common in folksongs.

My colleague, Bryan Stanley, and I followed a centuries-long tradition of art music composers creating new settings of folk material. Though the inevitable word "arrangement" is used to describe the settings, the approach to the work was fully compositional. Our aim was to compose an appropriate art song that is a fresh take on an old tune, designed for a classical singer and pianist. After searching through thousands of songs, we each chose those that sparked an individual musical imagination. Many American folksongs have only serviceable tunes, relying on a narrative of many verses to relate a compelling story. Another large number of folksongs are more instrumental in nature, essentially fiddle tunes for dancing. We skipped over these, attracted to more intriguing melodies.

After all the arrangements were completed it became apparent that we are both most often attracted to dramatic songs, rather than pastoral ones. There is an implied, strong character singing many of the songs we chose. Since we are both composers with somewhat theatrical temperaments, not only the core songs themselves, but also the settings we wrote tend to the dramatic.

American folksongs have some distinguishing qualities, and also share characteristics with folk tunes from other cultures. The vast West of the nineteenth century, and the consequential lives of its drifters, workers and settlers, are recurring themes. The loneliness of the hard life on isolated farms and ranches, or in the settlements and tiny towns of a predominantly rural nation echoes again and again. Even the bright songs sometimes seem self-conscious cheer to combat hardship. American folk tunes tend to be melodically simple, rhythmically straightforward and often modal. Sometimes they seem to be homespun imitations of Victorian parlor songs. As in most cultures, themes of nature and the countryside, of love and courtship ("Black Is the Color of My True Love's Hair," "Soldier, Soldier, Will You Marry Me," "I Gave My Love a Cherry," "Beware, Oh, Take Care," "Daughter, Will You Marry?," "Whistle, Daughter, Whistle," "The River in the Pines"), of the jilted lover ("Once I Had a Sweetheart"), of nonsense and silliness ("Bill Groggin's Goat"), and of men and women separated by war find frequent expression in American folksongs.

The songs in this collection date from the early eighteenth century to the early twentieth century. A few are American adaptations of British or Irish songs. There are war songs, love songs, sentimental ballads, poetic songs from Appalachia, comic songs, sea chanteys, work songs, and representation in song of the ultimate nineteenth-century icon of the American West, the cowboy.

In times prior to modern urban America, various aspects of religious life were interwoven into the daily experience of the population. It was later, in the twentieth century, that a view of culture developed that segregated the sacred and the secular. To represent the full spectrum of American folk material, sturdy sacred folk tunes are also included in this collection: "Amazing Grace" (an early American tune, though with words by a British author), "Come, Thou Fount of Every Blessing," "How Can I Keep from Singing," "How Firm a Foundation," "Wayfaring Stranger" and "Wondrous Love." African-American spirituals, songs of the slaves, are some of our richest American folksongs, here represented by "Let Us Break Bread Together" and "We Are Climbing Jacob's Ladder."

The bereft young woman left alone when her lover or husband goes off to war (possibly leaving her without adequate income and with few options for employment) was a universally recognized predicament for centuries, and is addressed in "Johnny Has Gone for a Soldier" and "The Cruel War Is Raging." The numbing experience of a horrific Civil War battle was captured in "The Battle on Shiloh's Hill." Life at sea undoubtedly had plenty of dull stretches that begged for lively chanteys like "Greenland Fisheries," "Haul Away, Joe" and "Sacramento." "The Banks of the Ohio" relays a notorious tale of passionate murder that could have been pulled from today's tabloid headlines; in folksong form it becomes a surprisingly frank yet sympathetic portrait of tragic jealousy. The monotonous, housebound life of women finds vivid, humored expression in "The Housewife's Lament" and "Single Girl."

Lonesome homesickness must have been a frequent ache of those who ventured west, heard in "Shenandoah" and "Nine Hundred Miles." The young cowboy whose rowdy, lone wolf life abruptly ends is immortalized in "The Streets of Laredo," surely one of the most powerfully sentimental of American songs. Monumental events are documented in folksongs, as in the account in "Mighty Day" of a devastating hurricane and flood in Galveston, Texas. The work-filled lives of farmers and ranchers were not perhaps conducive to lyrical renderings, since there are proportionately few songs about these topics. However, the full implications of the beginnings of a cholera epidemic among cattle are heard in the mournful dialogue song "Sail Around." "The Honest Ploughman" is a lighthearted yet nostalgic account of a poor farmer's lack of progress.

As composers who like singers and are drawn to writing vocal music, Bryan and I want each song to be as comfortable and as flattering as possible to the voice. Because each voice is an individual and unique instrument, each works a bit differently and has its own sweet spots of range and tessitura. Therefore, we have deliberately composed vocal options at selected points, generally where the highest or lowest notes can be avoided, yet allowing the piece to remain melodically satisfying. Sometimes the vocal options are not about extreme range, but about high, soft singing. Our message in the optional notes in these instances is that the dynamic is the most important musical detail. If the singer is struggling to sing the higher note softly, then she or he should choose to softly sing the more manageable, lower note.

There are many and various sources for American folksongs, often with differing word and melodic note content. This edition is not an attempt at creating a scholarly ethnomusicological source. We chose the versions that made the most sense to us as composers and used them freely. On rare occasions, we changed a word here or there to clarify intent or meaning for a modern audience.

These folksongs tell us about our American humanity. They are our stories in song, from our past and from our people, Americana in the truest and highest sense of the word. If you are an American, we hope that singing these songs is the discovery of a personal link to fellow citizens who have lived before you, be they lovers, soldiers, slaves, sailors, housewives, farmers, drifters, saints or sinners. And if you are not American, perhaps singing these folksongs will tell you something essential about who we are as a people.

Richard Walters
September, 2002

Amazing Grace

Early American Folk Melody
Words by John Newton (1725-1807)
arranged by Richard Walters

fear, And grace my fears re - lieved;_____ How prec - ious__

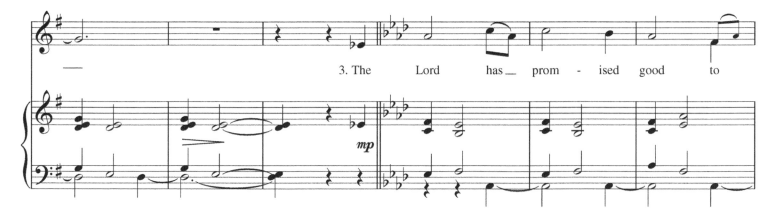

did that grace_____ ap - pear The__ hour I__ first be - lieved._____

— 3. The Lord has__ prom - ised good to

me His word my__ hope se - cures; He will_____ my__

*The singer is encouraged to embellish the melody; small notes are stylistic suggestions.

10

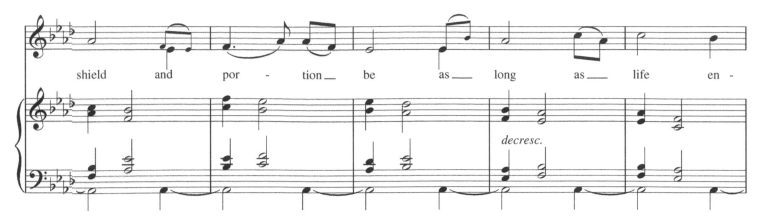

shield and por - tion be as long as life en -

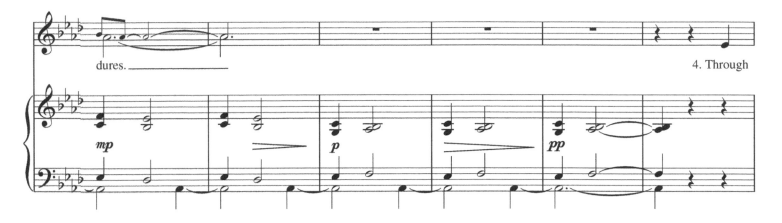

dures. 4. Through

man - y dan - gers toils and snares I have al -

read - y come; 'Tis grace hath brought me

safe ___ thus ___ far, And grace will ___ lead me home. ___

5. Yea, when this ___

flesh and heart shall fail, And mor - tal ___ life shall

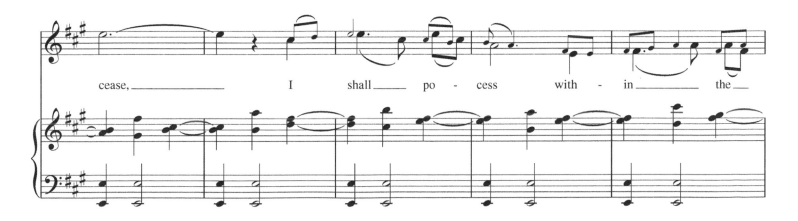

cease, ___ I shall ___ po - cess with - in ___ the ___

veil, a life of __ joy and peace. _____ 6. When

More Broadly

we've been __ there ten thou - sand __ years, bright shin - ing __ as the

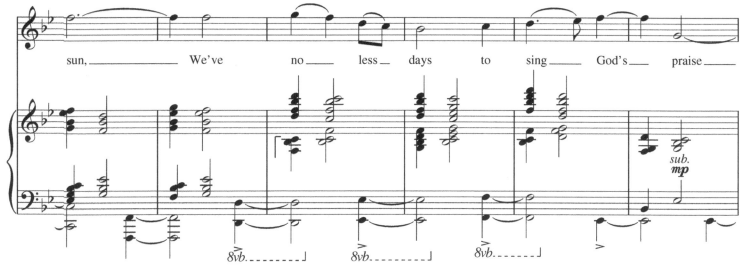

sun, _____ We've no __ less __ days to sing __ God's __ praise __

Than __ when _____ we first be

gun. _____

Was blind _____ but now I see. _____

* A third vocal line option:

Than __ when _____ we first be - gun. _____

The Banks of the Ohio

19th Century Midwestern American Folksong
arranged by Richard Walters

down by the banks _____ of the O - hi - o.

2. Please, on - ly ___ say _____ that you'll be ___ mine,

in no oth - er ___ arms _____ will you en - twine.

Down be - side _____ where the wa - ters flow,

down by the banks _____ of the O - hi - o. _____

3. She bowed her head _____ and turned a - way.

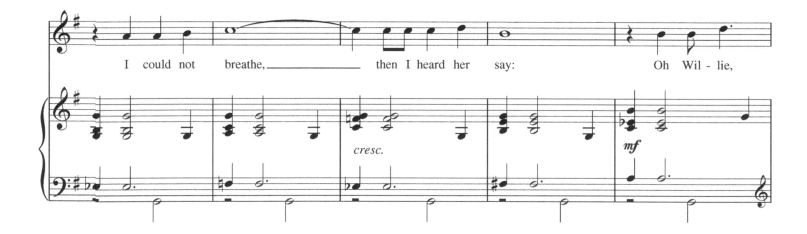

I could not breathe, _____ then I heard her say: Oh Wil - lie,

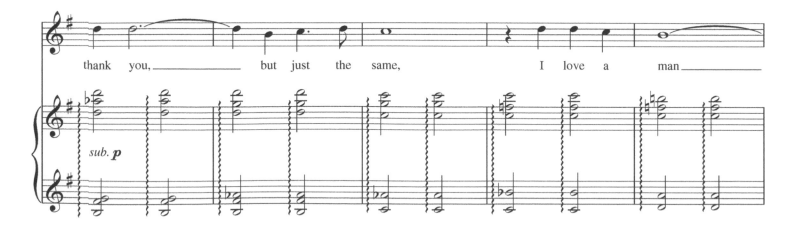

thank you, _____ but just the same, I love a man _____

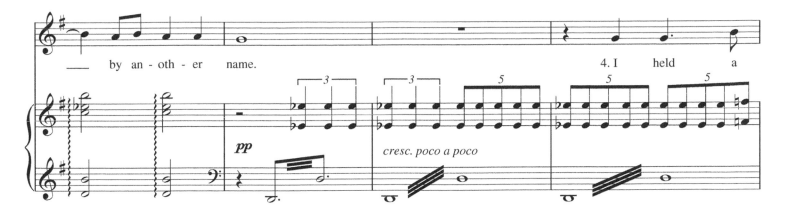

_____ by an - oth - er name.   4. I held a

knife   a - gainst her breast,   in - to my

arms_____ her bod - y pressed.   She begged, "Oh,

Wil - lie,_____ don't mur - der me,   I'm not pre -

(starkly)

The Battle on Shiloh's Hill

American Folksong from the Civil War
arranged by Bryan Stanley

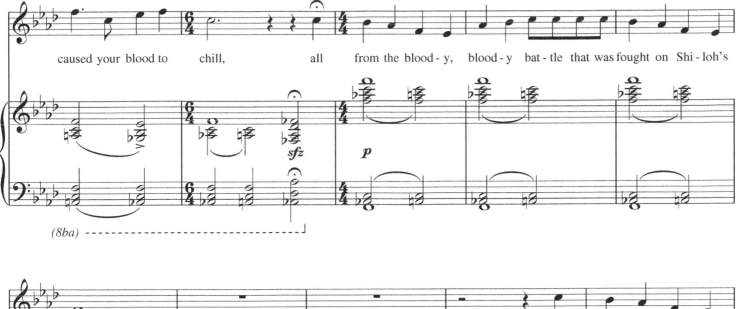

caused your blood to chill, all from the blood-y, blood-y bat-tle that was fought on Shi-loh's

Hill. 2. 'Twas on the sixth of

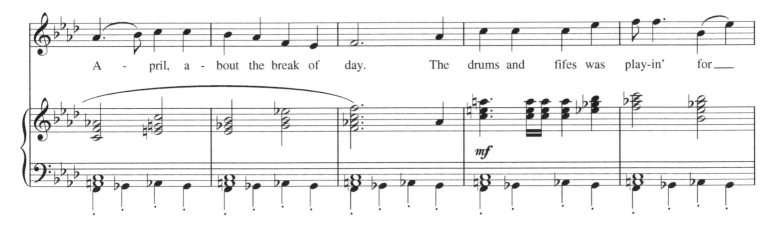

A - pril, a - bout the break of day. The drums and fifes was play-in' for ___

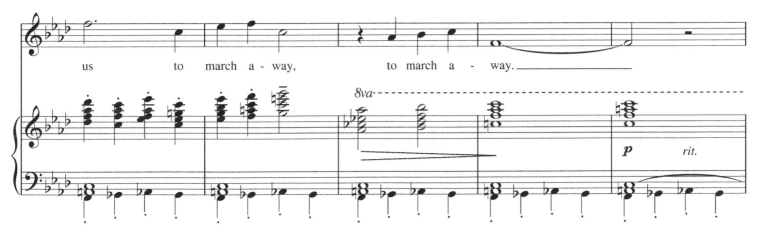

us to march a - way, to march a - way. ___

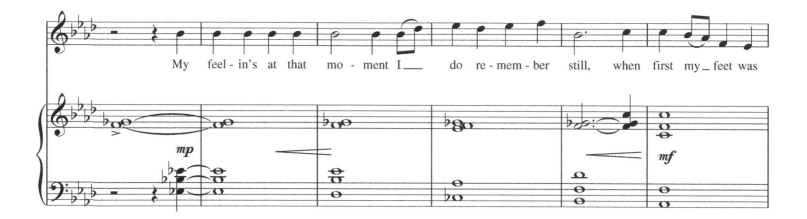

My feel - in's at that mo - ment I __ do re - mem - ber still, when first my __ feet was

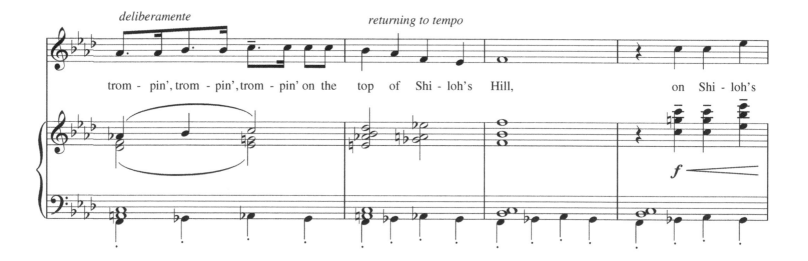

trom - pin', trom - pin', trom - pin' on the top of Shi - loh's Hill, on Shi - loh's

Hill! _____

23

3. A - bout the hour of sun - rise ____ the bat - tle first be - gan.

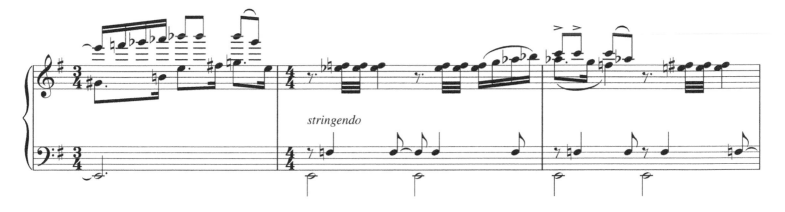

stringendo

Con più moto ♩ = 116

Be -

fore the day was en - ded, ____ we ___ fought ____ 'em hand to hand. The

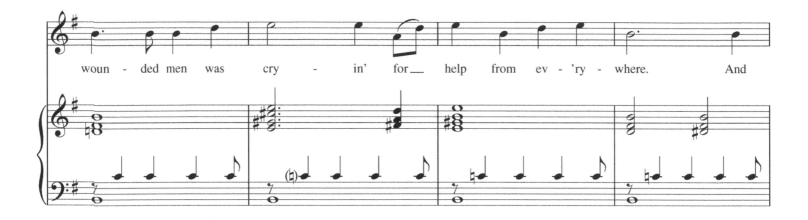

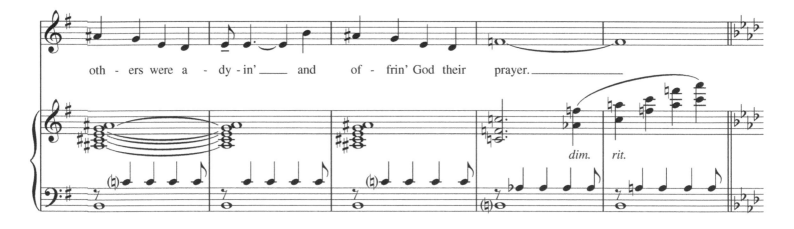

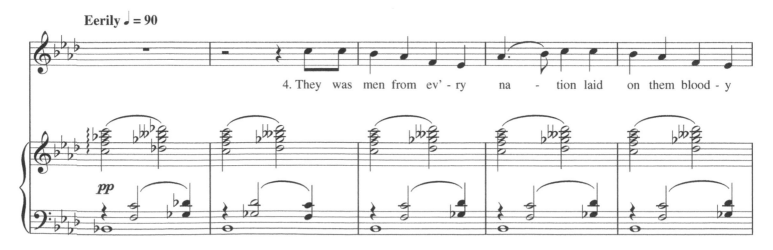

24

hor - rors of that bat - tle did my soul with an - guish fill. The

woun - ded men was cry - in' for ___ help from ev - 'ry - where. And

oth - ers were a - dy - in' ___ and of - frin' God their prayer. ___

Eerily ♩ = 90

4. They was men from ev' - ry na - tion laid on them blood - y

plains. They was fath - ers, sons and broth - ers, hus - bands and lov - ers brave, all

laid thick on the war - torn field that night on Shi - loh's Hill.

opt.

8va---

marcato
sub. f

Agitato ♩ = 108

♪ = ♪

(8va)

5. Ver - y ear - ly the next mor - nin' we were called to arms a - gain,

Pesante ♩ = 88

un - mind - ful of the woun - ded, un -

f

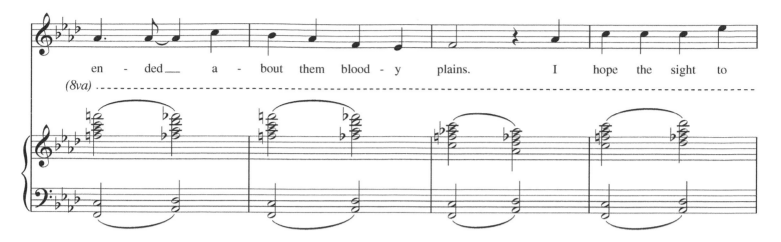

en - ded___ a - bout them blood - y plains. I hope the sight to

(8va)

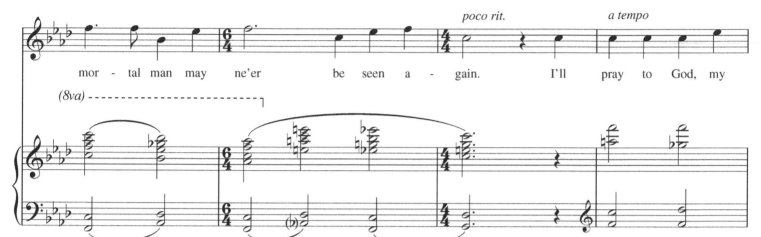

poco rit.   *a tempo*

mor - tal man may ne'er be seen a - gain. I'll pray to God, my

(8va)

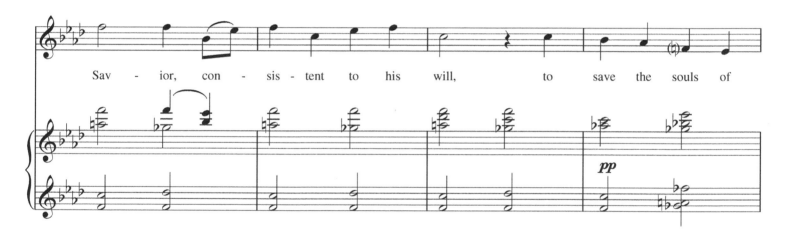

Sav - ior, con - sis - tent to his will, to save the souls of

pp

meno

them brave men who fell on Shi - loh's Hill.

pp

8ba

Beware, Oh, Take Care

19th Century American Folksong
arranged by Richard Walters

ware, young la-dies, they're fool-in' you. Be - ware, oh, take care.

2. A - round their neck they wear a guard. Be - ware, oh, take care. And

in their pock - et is a deck of cards. Be - ware, oh, take care. Be -

ware, young la - dies, they're fool-in' you. Trust them not, they're fool-in you. Be -

ware, young la - dies, they're fool - in' you. Be - ware, oh, take care.

3. They smoke, they chew, they wear fine shoes. Be -

ware, oh, take care. And in their pock - et is a bot - tle o' booze. Be -

ware, oh, take care. Be - ware, young la - dies, they're fool - in' you.

Trust them not, they're fool - in' you. Be - ware, young la - dies, they're fool - in' you. Be -

ware, oh, take care.

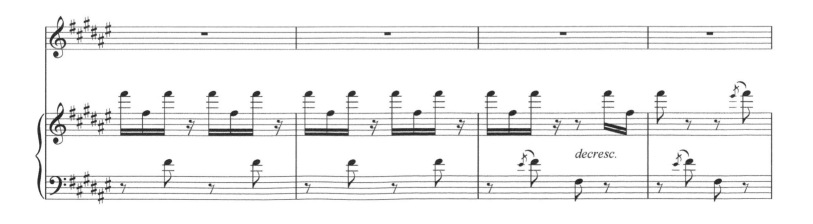

32

hold their hands up to their heart. They sigh, oh, they sigh. _____ They

say they love no one but you. _____ They lie, oh, they

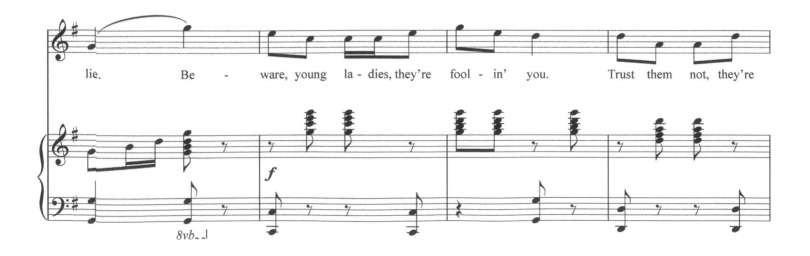

lie. Be - ware, young la - dies, they're fool - in' you. Trust them not, they're

8vb

fool - in' you. Be - ware, young la - dies, they're fool - in' you. Be - ware, oh, take

care. Be - ware, oh, take care. Be - ware! Be -

ware! Be - ware! Be - ware! _____

Be - ware, oh, take care! _____

Bill Groggin's Goat

Southern Appalachian Folksong
arranged by Richard Walters

goat, _____ in - deed he did,

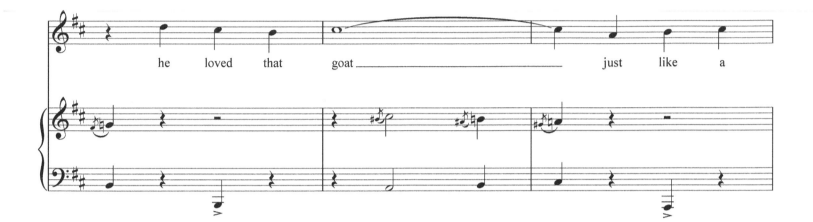

he loved that goat _____ just like a

kid.   2. One day the

goat _____ felt frisk and fine,   ate three red

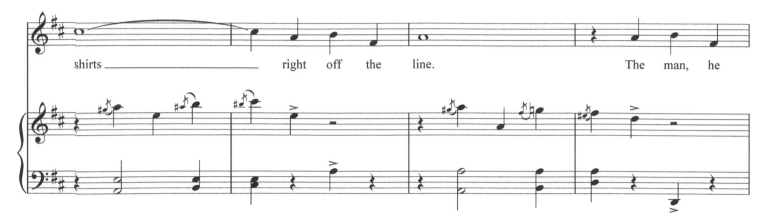

shirts _____ right off the line. The man, he

grabbed _____ him by the back _____ and tied him

to _____ a rail - road track.

3. Now, when the train _____ came in - to

sight, _____ that goat grew pale _____ and green with

fright. He heaved a sigh _____ as if in

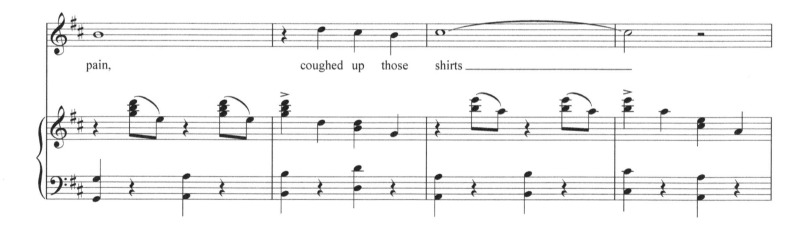

pain, coughed up those shirts _____

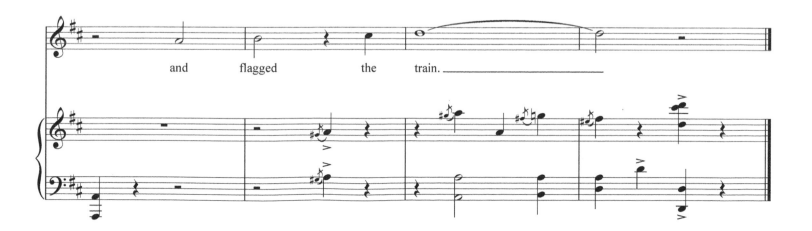

and flagged the train. _____

Black Is the Color of My True Love's Hair

Southern Appalachian Folksong
arranged by Bryan Stanley

Slowly, freely at first *a tempo* ♩ = 60

1. Black, black, black is the col-or of my true love's hair. Her

lips _____ are like a rose so fair. And the

pret-ti-est face and the neat-est_ hands. I love_____ the grass where

poco rit.

a tempo

on she stands, she with the won - drous hair.

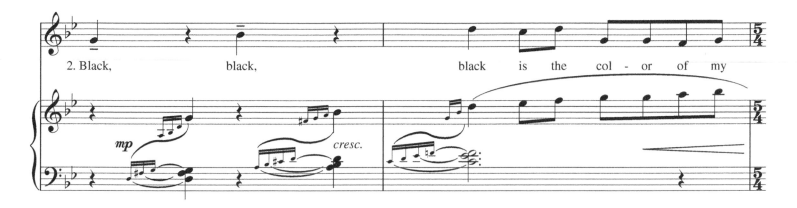

2. Black, black, black is the col - or of my

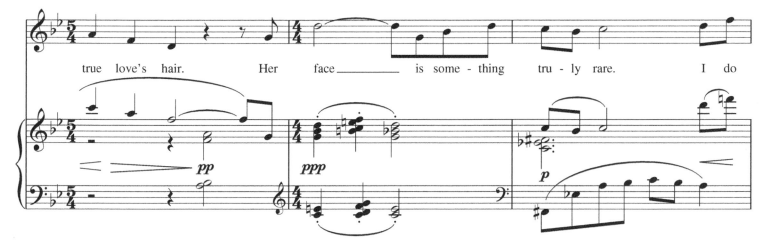

true love's hair. Her face_____ is some - thing tru - ly rare. I do

love my_ love, and so well_ she_ knows._ I love_____ the ground where

she walks by, she with the won - drous hair.____

3. Black, black,

black is the col - or of my true love's hair.

A -

Con più moto ♩ = 94

lone_____ my life would be so bare.____ I would

sigh,   I would weep,   I would nev - er fall a -

returning to Tempo I

sleep.   My   love _____   is way be -

Tempo I

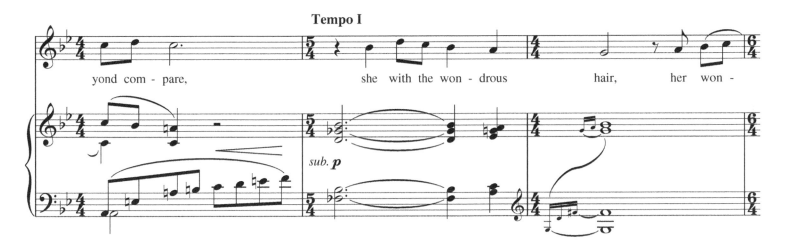

yond com - pare,   she with the won - drous   hair,   her won -

- drous   hair, _____ her   won - drous   hair.

Bury Me Beneath the Willow

Southeastern American Folksong
arranged by Bryan Stanley

'Neath the weep-ing wil-low tree. And when ⎧he⎫ knows where I am sleep-ing,
⎩she⎭

then per - haps ⎧he'll⎫ weep for me. 2. They
⎩she'll⎭

told me that ⎧he⎫ loved an - oth - er, I could not be-lieve them true un -
⎩she⎭

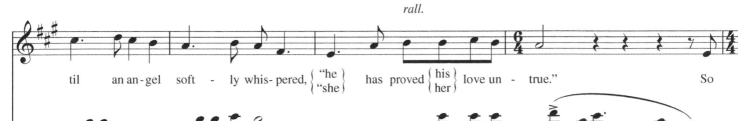

til an an-gel soft - ly whis-pered, ⎧"he⎫ has proved ⎧his⎫ love un - true." So
⎩"she⎭ ⎩her⎭

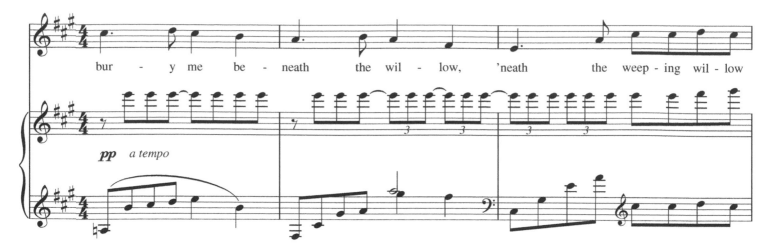

bur - y me be - neath the wil - low, 'neath the weep - ing wil - low

tree, and when {he}{she} knows where I am sleep - ing then per - haps {he'll}{she'll} weep for

me. 3. To - mor - row was to be our wed - ding

Lord, oh Lord where can {he}{she} be? {He's}{She's} gone a - way to

wed an-oth-er; {he}{she} no lon-ger cares for me. So

Tempo I

bur-y me, oh bur-y me 'neath the weep-ing wil-low tree And

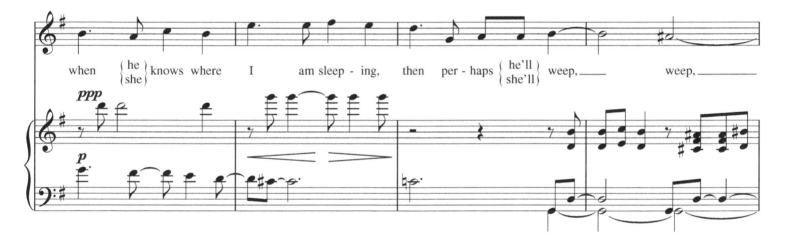

when {he}{she} knows where I am sleep-ing, then per-haps {he'll}{she'll} weep,_____ weep,_____

——— weep, for me.___

for Kimm

Come, Thou Fount
of Every Blessing

Robert Robinson, 1758

American Folk Tune
First set by John Wyeth, 1813
arranged by Richard Walters

flam - ing tongues a - bove; Praise the mount! I'm fixed up - on it, Mount of

Thy re - deem-ing love. Here I

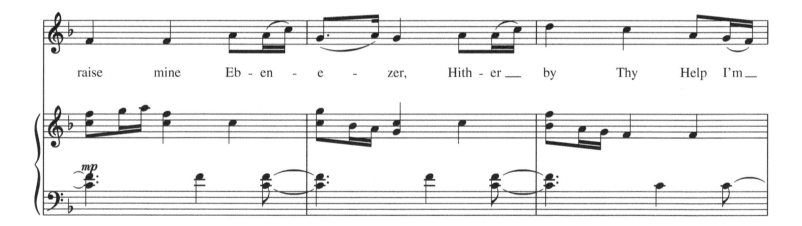

raise mine Eb - en - e - zer, Hith - er by Thy Help I'm

come; And I hope, by Thy good pleas - ure, Safe - ly

to ar - rive at _ home. Je - sus _ sought me when a stran - ger, Wan-der-ing

cresc.

from the fold of __ God; He, to ___ res - cue me from __

f *mp*

dan - ger, In - ter - posed his pre - cious _ blood. O to __

f

grace how great a debt - or Dai - ly __ I'm con - strained to

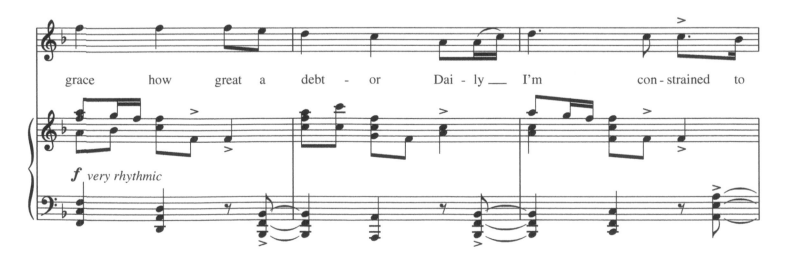

f very rhythmic

49

The Cruel War Is Raging

American Folksong from the Civil War
arranged by Richard Walters

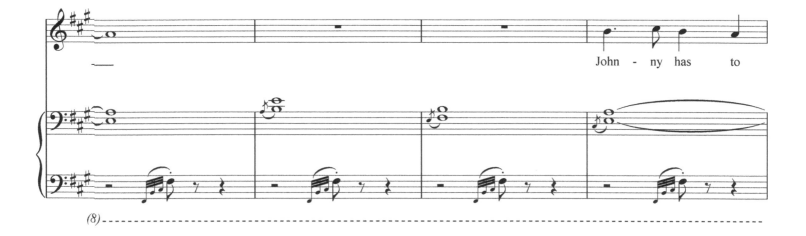

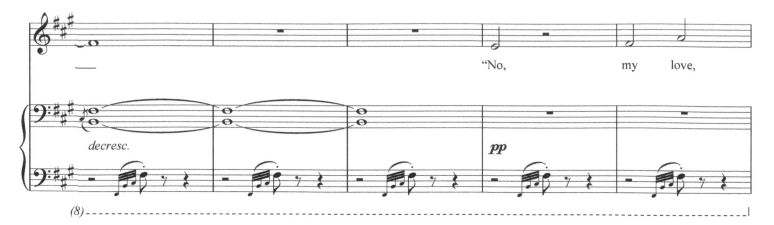

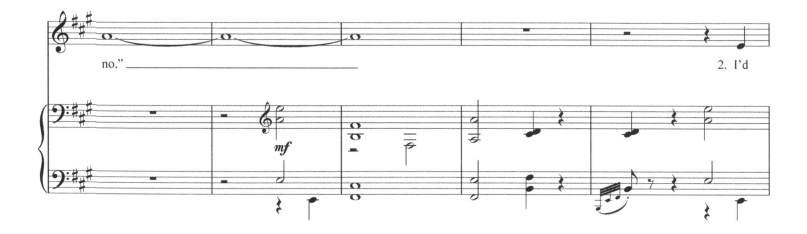

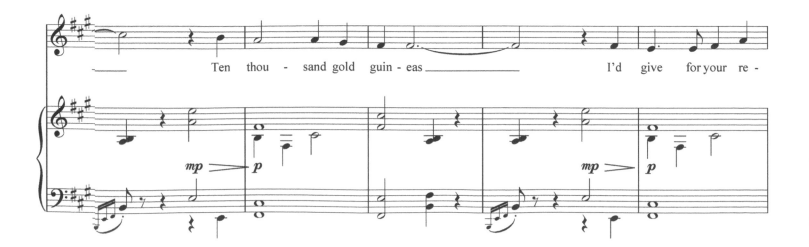

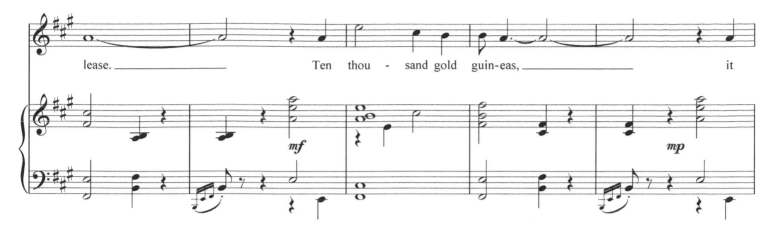

lease._____ Ten thou - sand gold guin-eas,_____ it

grieves__ my heart so._____ Won't you let me go with you?_____

"No, my love, no."

3. To - mor - row is__

Sun - day, Mon - day is the day your cap - tain will call you and

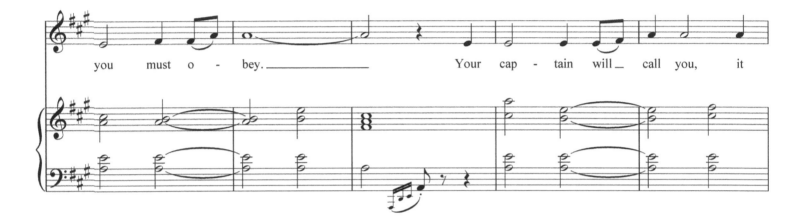

you must o - bey. _____ Your cap - tain will_ call you, it

grieves_ my heart so. Won't you_ let me go with you? "No, my love,

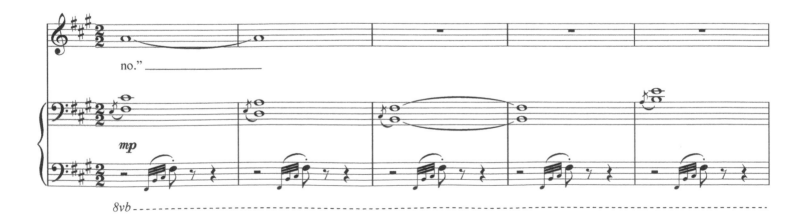

no." _____

8vb

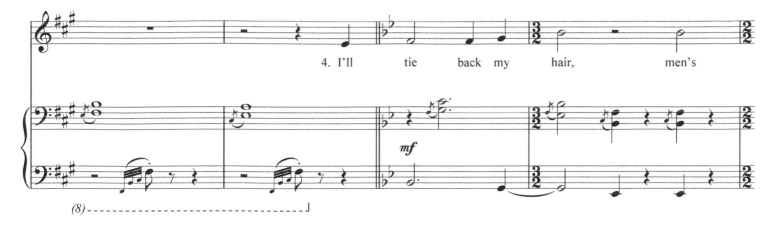

4. I'll tie back my hair, men's

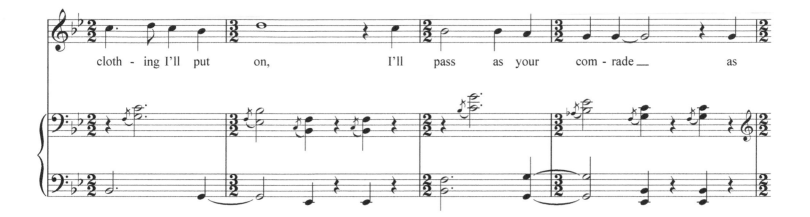

cloth - ing I'll put on, I'll pass as your com - rade as

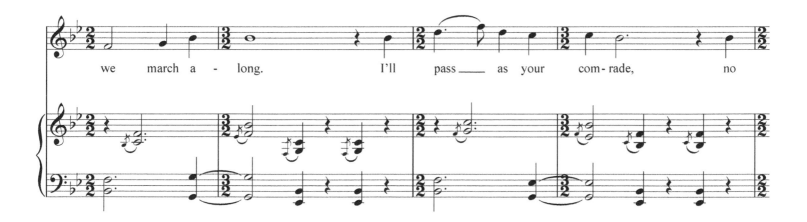

we march a - long. I'll pass as your com - rade, no

one will ev - er know. Won't you let me go with you?

"No, my love." No! _____

Andante espressivo ♩ = 88

5. John - ny, oh, John - ny, I fear you are un -

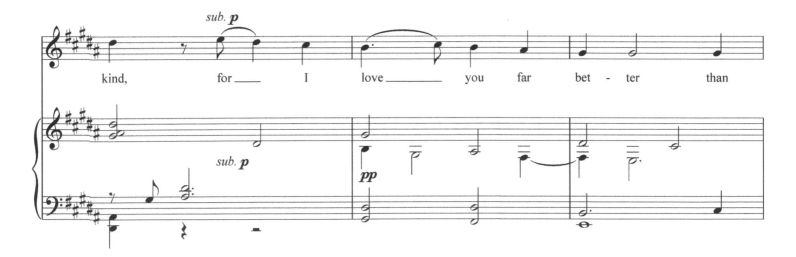

kind, for ___ I love _____ you far bet - ter than

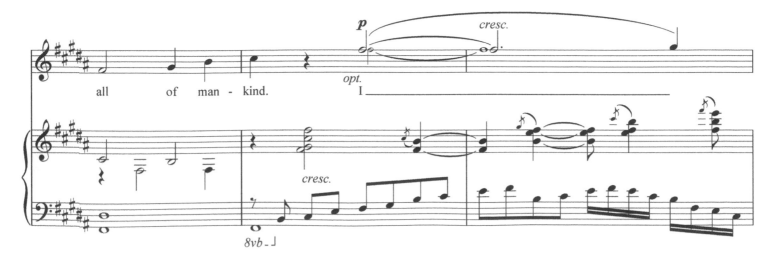

all of man - kind. I _____

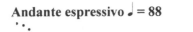

love _____ you far bet - ter than words can e'er ex - press. Won't you

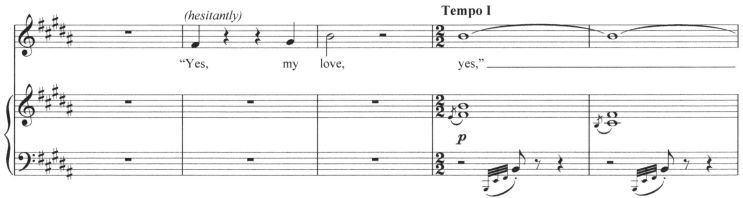

let me go with you?

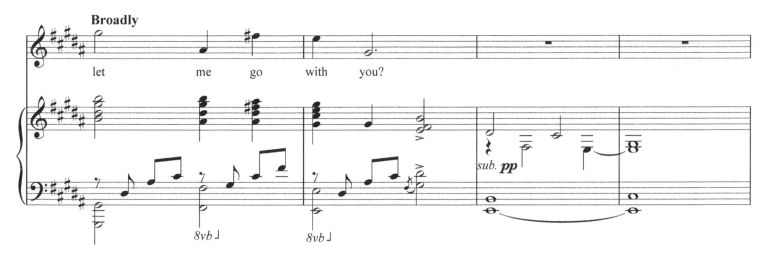

"Yes, my love, yes," _____

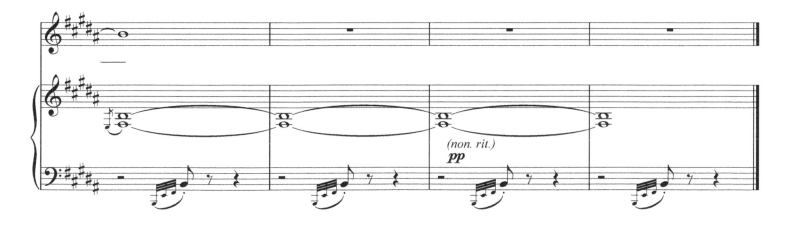

* another option

love _____ you far

Daughter, Will You Marry?

Pennsylvania Dutch folksong
arranged by Bryan Stanley

1. "Daugh-ter, will you mar - ry?"
2. "Daugh-ter, will you mar - ry?"

"Yea, fa - ther, yea!" "Will you mar-ry a farm - er?"
"Yea, fa - ther, yea!" "Will you mar-ry a preach - er?"

"Nay, fa - ther, nay! Mar - ry a farm - er, no, I'll not; clean - ing a sta - ble's not my lot!
"Nay, fa - ther, nay! Mar - ry a preach - er, no, my dear; I'd rock the cra - dle ev - 'ry year!

Nay, fa - ther, nay!"   Nay, fa - ther, nay!"

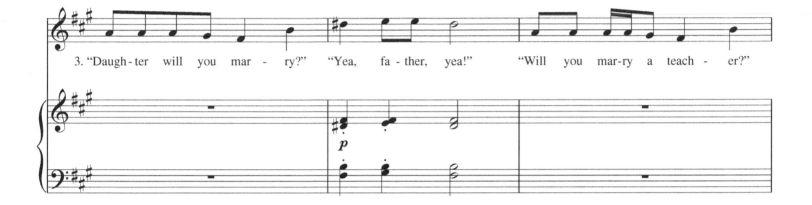

3. "Daugh - ter will you mar - ry?" "Yea, fa - ther, yea!" "Will you mar-ry a teach - er?"

"Nay, fa - ther, nay! I could-n't be a teach-er's wife, scream-ing kids would shor - ten my life!

Nay, father, nay."   4. "Daugh - ter will you mar - ry?"

"Yea, fa - ther, yea." "Will you mar - ry a doc - tor?

"Nay, fa - ther, nay! Doc - tor's wife I will not be; poi - son - ing peo - ple's not for me!

Nay, fa -ther, nay!"

5. "Will you mar-ry a law - yer?" "Nay fa - ther, nay." 6. "Will you mar-ry a shoe - mak - er?"

"Nay, fa -ther, nay! Mar - ry a shoe - mak - er, no no no, I'd be waxed from head to toe!

Nay, fa - ther, nay!" 7. "O' Daugh - ter, will you mar - ry?"

"Yea, fa - ther, yea." "Will you mar-ry a car - pen - ter?" "Nay, fa - ther, nay.

I can't do a thing like that where pound - ing nails go tap tap tap! Nay, fa - ther, nay!"

Slower

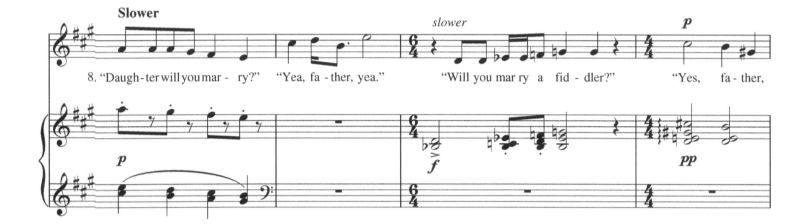

8, "Daugh-ter will you mar - ry?" "Yea, fa - ther, yea." "Will you mar ry a fid - dler?" "Yes, fa - ther,

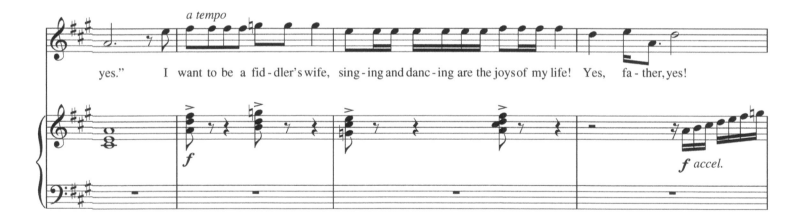

yes." I want to be a fid - dler's wife, sing - ing and danc - ing are the joys of my life! Yes, fa - ther, yes!

Allegro assai

The Housewife's Lament

American Folksong
arranged by Bryan Stanley

beau - ty will fade___ and rich - es will flee. Pleasures, they dwin - dle and

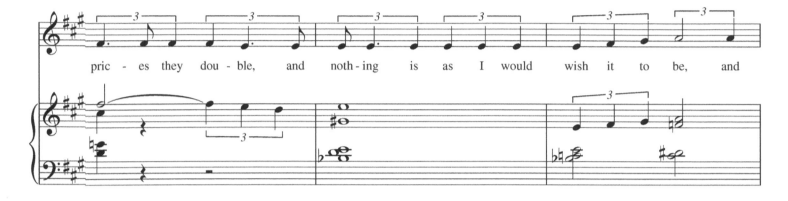

pric - es they dou - ble, and noth - ing is as I would wish it to be, and

noth - ing___ is as I would wish it to be.

2. There's too much of wor - ry that goes to a bon - net, there's

too much of i - ron - ing that goes in - to a shirt. There's noth - ing that pays for the

time you waste on it, there's noth - ing that lasts us but trou - ble and dirt.

3. In March there is mud, it is slush in De - cem - ber, the mid-sum - mer breez-es are

load-ed with dust. In fall, the leaves lit - ter, and mud - dy Sep-tem-ber, the wall-pa-per rots and the

can - dle - sticks rust. Life is a toil __ and love is a trou - ble, __

beau - ty will fade __ and rich - es will flee. Pleas ures, they dwin - dle and

pri - ces they dou - ble, and noth - ing is as I would wish it to be, and

noth - ing __ is as I would wish it to be.

Presto

4. There are worms on the cher - ries and slugs on the ro - ses and ants in the sug - ar and mice in the pies. The

rub - bish of spi - ders no mor - tal sup - pos - es, and rav - ag - ing roa - ches and dam - ag - ing flies. 5. It's

sweep - in' at six and it's dust - in' at sev - en, it's vic - tuals at eight and it's dish - es at nine,

pot - tin' and pan - nin' from ten to e - lev - en, we scarce break our fast till we plan how to dine.

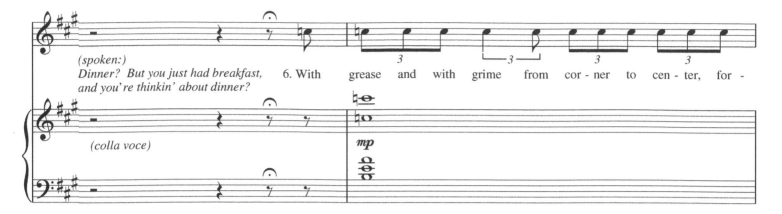

(spoken:)
Dinner? But you just had breakfast,
and you're thinkin' about dinner?

(colla voce)

6. With grease and with grime from cor-ner to cen-ter, for-

mp

ev-er at war and for-ev-er a-lert. No rest for a day lest the en-e-my en-ter. I

rit.

Tempo primo

spend my whole life in the strug-gle with dirt. Ah!_____

cresc.

mf

f

Life is a toil____ and

mp

beau - ty will fade. Pleas - ures, they dwin - dle and pric - es they dou - ble _ and

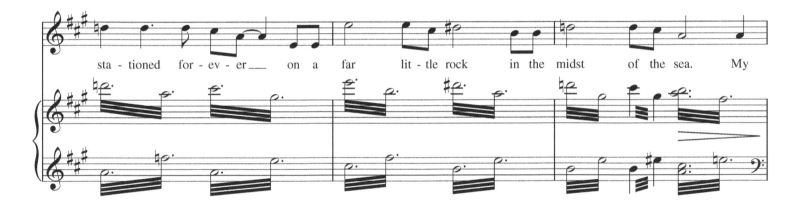

noth-ing is as I would wish it to be. 7. Last night in my dreams I was

sta - tioned for - ev - er _ on a far lit - tle rock in the midst of the sea. My

one change in life was a cease - less en - deav - or to sweep off the waves as they _ swept o - ver me."

Tempo primo

But it was no dream,___ a-head I be-hold it. I see I am help-less my fate to a-vert.

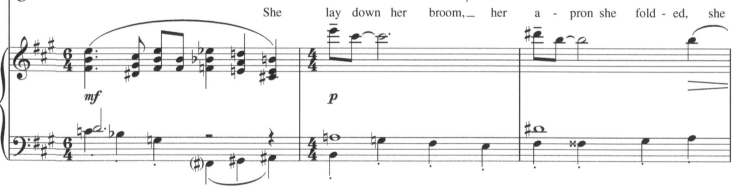

She lay down her broom,___ her a-pron she fold-ed, she

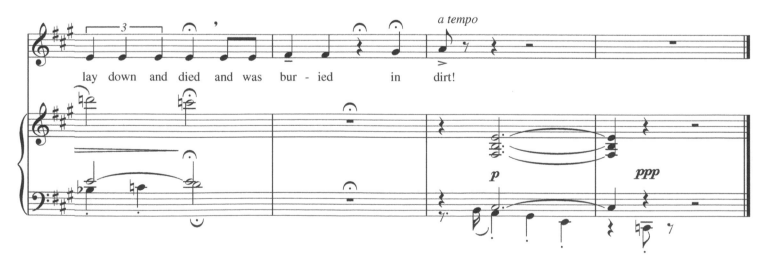

lay down and died and was bur-ied in dirt!

a tempo

The Honest Ploughman

American Folksong
arranged by Bryan Stanley

3. To drive the plough, my fa - ther did a boy en - gage, un -

til that I had just ar - rived at sev - en years of age. So then he did no ser - vant want, my

moth - er milked the cow. And___ with the lark I rose each morn to go and drive the plough.

4. When I was fif - teen years of age, I used to thrash and sow, I___

length when I was twen - ty five, I took my - self a wife, com -

keep a pig and cow. She could sit and knit, and spin,_____ and
ban - ished pain and grief. We had not oc - ca - sion then_ to _ ask for

I the land could plough. There noth - ing was up - on a farm at
par - ish re - lief. But now my hairs are grown quite grey, I

all but I can do. I_____ feel things ver - y diff - 'rent now_ that's
can - not well en - gage to_____ work as I had used to do I'm

1
man - y years a - go. 7. We

2 *allarg.*
nine - ty years of _ age. 8. When a

slower **Lamentóso ♩ = 60**
man has la - bored all his life, to

colla voce   *rit.*   ***p*** *espress.*

do his coun-try good, he's re - spect-ed just as much as a don-key in a wood. His

Even slower ♩ = 56

days are gone and past, and he may weep in grief and woe. The ___ times are ver - y diff - 'rent now, to

rit.   *a tempo*   *rall.*

nine - ty years a - go, to nine - ty years a - go, to nine - ty years a -

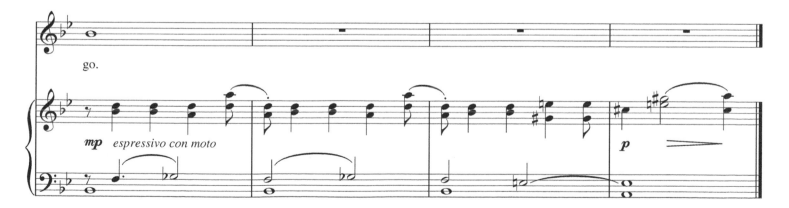

go.

mp espressivo con moto

Greenland Fisheries/Haul Away, Joe

American Sea Chanteys
arranged by Bryan Stanley

1. T'was in eigh-teen hun-dred and fif-ty three, and of June the thir-teenth__ day, that our gal-lant ship her__ an-chor__weighed, and for Green-land bore__ a-

way, brave boys, and for Green-land bore_ a_way.

'Way, haul a-way,_ we'll haul for fin - er wind and weath-er. 'Way haul a-

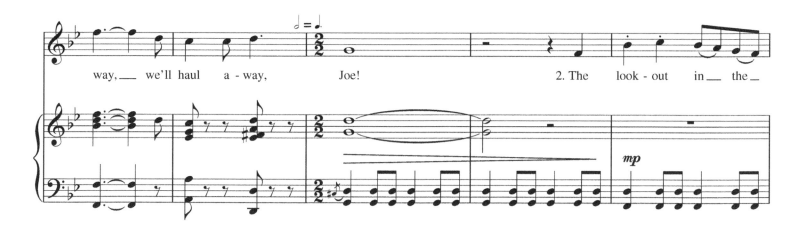

way,_ we'll haul a-way, Joe! 2. The look-out in the_

cross-tree stood with a spy-glass in_ his_ hand. "There's a whale, there's a whale, there's a

78

whale - fish," he cried, "and she blows at ev - 'ry___ span, brave boys, brave boys, she___

blows,___ she___ blows,_____ blows,_____ She___

blows at ev - 'ry span! Way, haul a - way,_____ we'll

haul for fin - er wind and weath - er. 'Way, haul a - way,_____ we'll

haul a - way, Joe! 3. Now the boats were launched and the

men a - board, the whale in full view; re - solved, was each

sea - man bold to steer where the whale - fish blew, brave boys, brave boys, brave boys, to

steer where she blew. There she blows, there she blows, there she blows.

We did steer where she blew.

'Way, haul a-way, we'll haul her through the wind and rain. 'Way, haul her a-

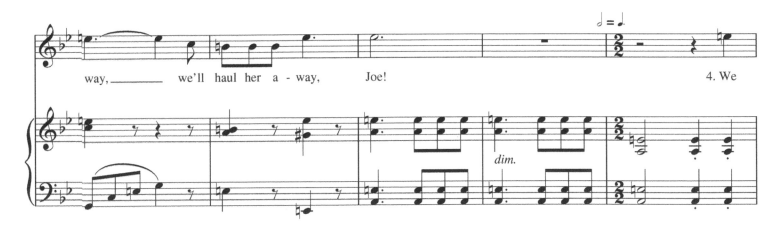

way, we'll haul her a-way, Joe! 4. We

struck that whale, the line paid out, then a flour-ish of his

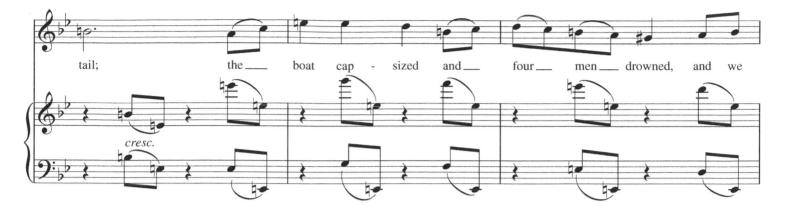

tail;   the___ boat cap - sized and___ four___ men___ drowned, and we

largando, solemnly   *rit.*

nev - er caught___ that___ whale,   brave boys,   brave boys,   brave boys,   brave boys...

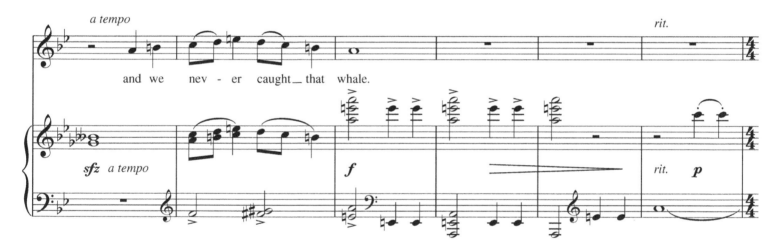

a tempo   *rit.*

and we   nev - er caught___ that whale.

Meno ♩ = 86

5. "To lose that whale,"___ our___ cap - tain said, "it___ grieves my heart___ full___

sore; but _ lose four gal - lant _ hear - ted men, it _ grieves me ten _ times _ more, it _

Tempo primo

grieves _ me ten _ times more. _____

6. Oh, Green - land is _ a _ dread - ful place, a _ land that's nev - er _ green, where there's

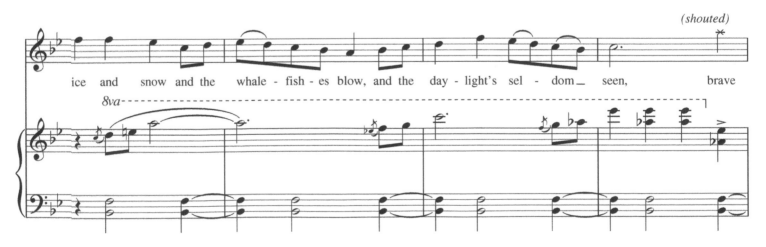

ice and snow and the whale - fish - es blow, and the day - light's sel - dom _ seen, brave

boys! The_ day-light's far a - way,_____

'Way, haul a - way,_____ we'll haul for warm - er, sun - ny weath - er. 'Way, haul a-

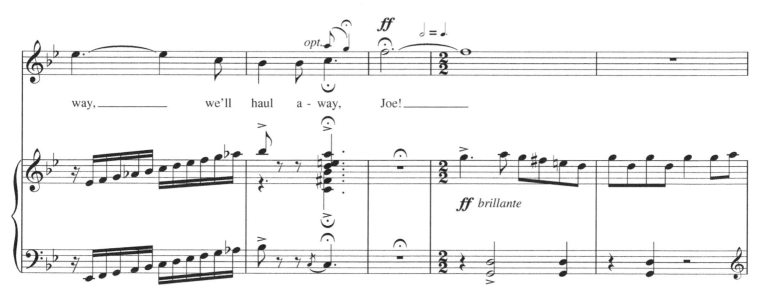

way,_____ we'll haul a - way, Joe!_____

for Carol and Anne

How Can I Keep from Singing

(duet)

American Folksong
Arranged by Richard Walters

85

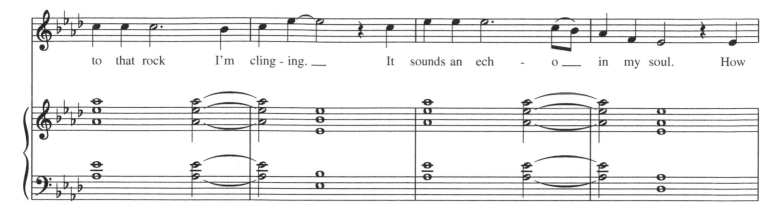

to that rock I'm cling-ing. __ It sounds an ech - o __ in my soul. How

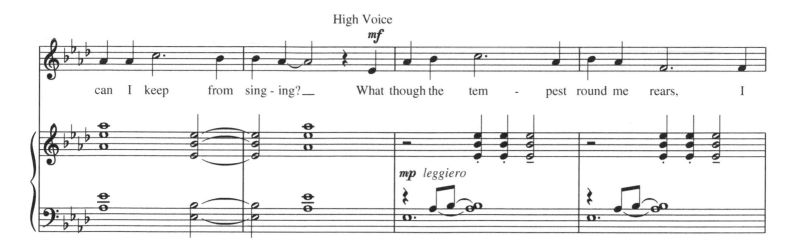

High Voice
mf
can I keep from sing-ing? __ What though the tem - pest round me rears, I
mp leggiero

know the truth, it liv-eth. __ What though the dark - ness round me close, Songs

in the night it giv-eth. __ No storm can shake my in-most calm while
8va

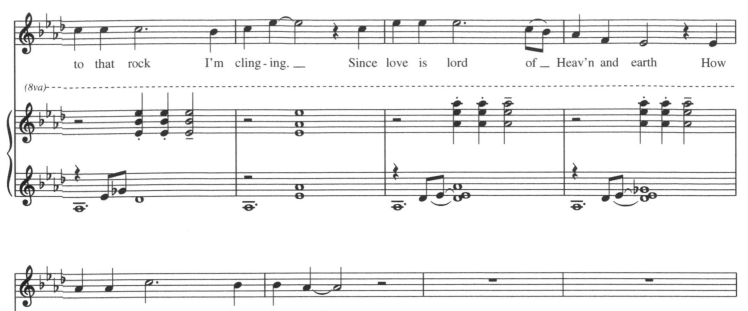

to that rock I'm cling-ing. ___ Since love is lord of ___ Heav'n and earth How

can I keep from sing-ing? ___

High Voice

When ty-rants trem - ble, sick with fear _____ And hear their death knells

Medium Voice

When ty-rants trem - ble, sick with fear And hear their death knells

like a sturdy hymn

88

Slower to the end

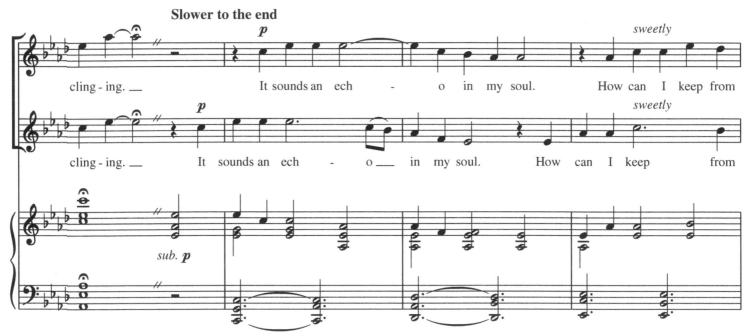

How Can I Keep from Singing

American Folksong
arranged by Richard Walters

Allegretto; steady

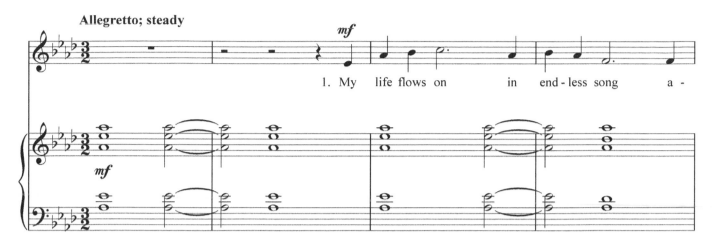

1. My life flows on in end-less song a-

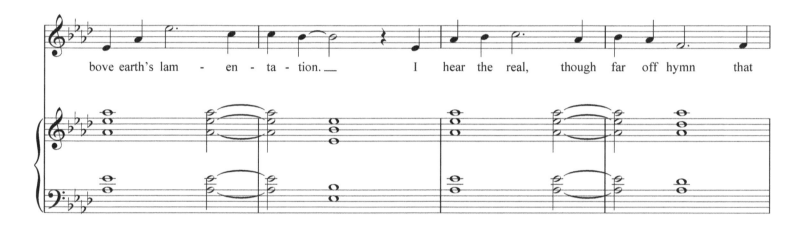

bove earth's lam - en - ta - tion. __ I hear the real, though far off hymn that

hails a new cre - a - tion. __ No storm can shake my in - most calm while

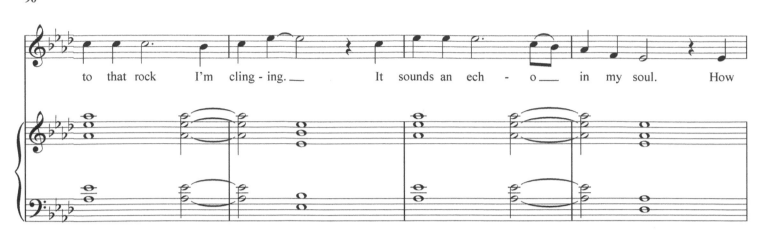

to that rock I'm cling-ing.___ It sounds an ech - o___ in my soul. How

can I keep from sing-ing?___ 2. What though the tem - pest round me rears, I

know the truth, it liv-eth.___ What though the dark - ness round me close, Songs

in the night it giv-eth.___ No storm can shake my in-most calm while

to that rock I'm cling-ing.__ Since love is lord of__ Heav'n and earth How

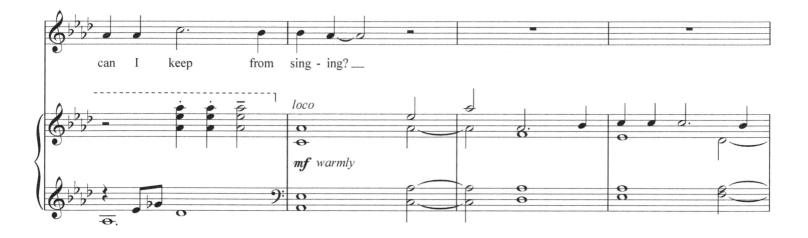

can I keep from sing-ing?__

loco

mf warmly

mf

3. When ty-rants trem - ble, sick with fear And hear their death knells

like a sturdy hymn

ring - ing; — When friends re - joice both far and near, How can I keep from

sing - ing? — In pris - on cell and dun - geon vile Our thoughts to them are

wing - ing. When friends by shame are — un - de - filed, How can I keep from

93

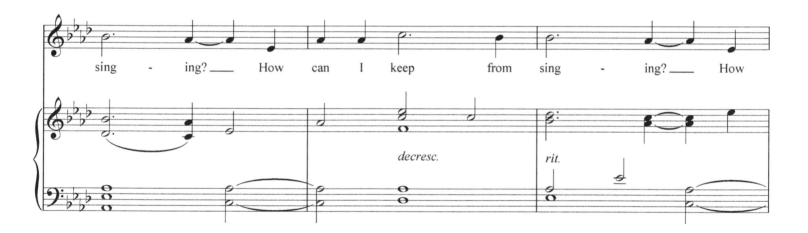

for Russ and Rose Marie

How Firm A Foundation

John Rippon's *A Selection of Hymns*, 1787

Early American Melody
arranged by Richard Walters

ex - cel - lent word! What more can he say than to

you he hath said, To ___ you who for ref - uge to

Je - sus have fled?

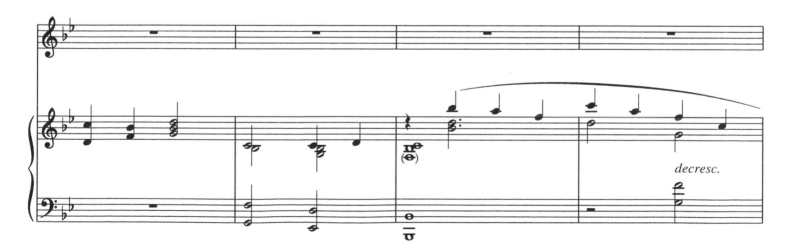

Fear ____ not I am with thee, oh

be not dis - mayed, For ____ I am thy God and will

still give thee aid. I'll strength - en thee, help thee, and

cause thee to stand, Up - held by my right - eous om -

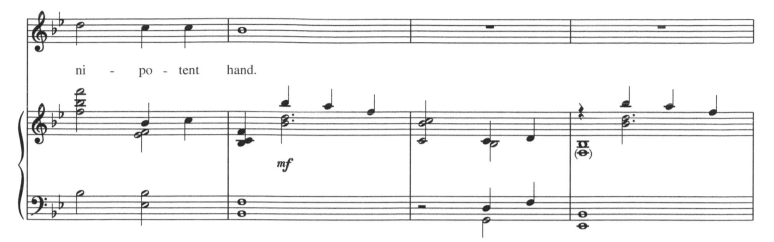

ni - po - tent hand.

mf

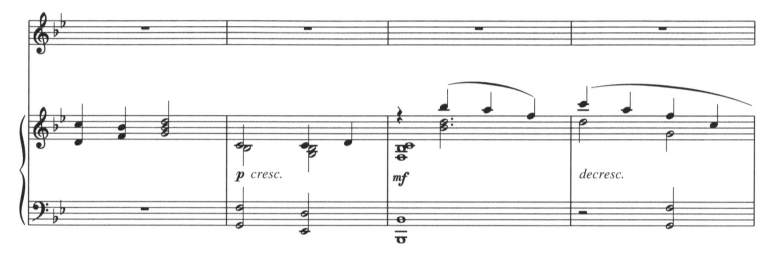

p cresc.   *mf*   decresc.

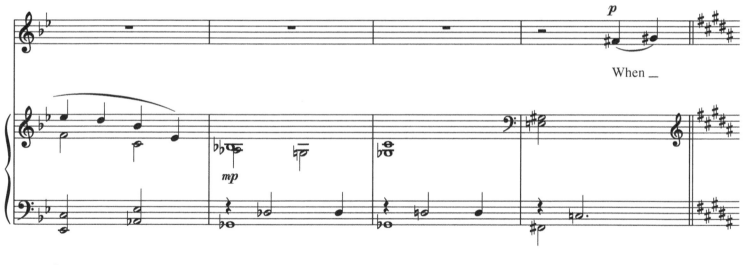

p

When ___

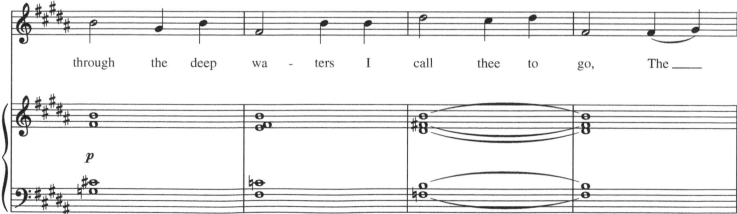

through   the   deep   wa - ters   I   call   thee   to   go,   The ___

p

riv - ers of woe shall not thee o - ver - flow; For

I will be near thee, thy trou - bles to bless, And

sanc - ti - fy to thee thy deep - est dis - tress.

mp

99

More broadly

soul   that   on   Je - sus   hath   leaned   for   re - pose   I

rit.

opt.

will not, I will not des - sert to his foes,

rit.

Slower to the end

opt.

That soul, though all hell _____ should en - deav - or to

ff

dolce

8vb   *8vb*

p

shake, I'll _____ nev - er, no ne -

p

Tempo primo

f

ver, No, nev - er for - sake. _____

8va -

p   *f*

8vb

Once I Had a Sweetheart

Southern Appalachian Folksong
arranged by Richard Walters

gone and left __ me, he's gone and left __ me. He's

gone and leaves __ me to sor - row and

moan. _____ 2. He was such a

sweet - heart, oh, hap - py hours! _____

When it was my birth - day, he brought me

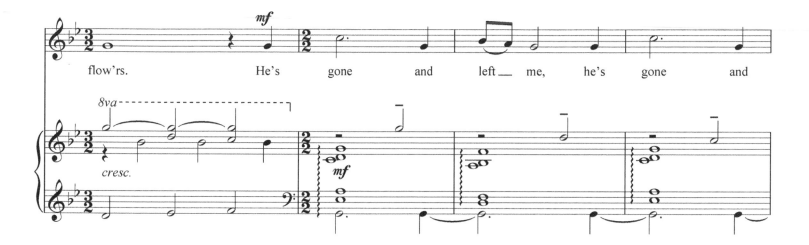

flow'rs. He's gone and left __ me, he's gone and

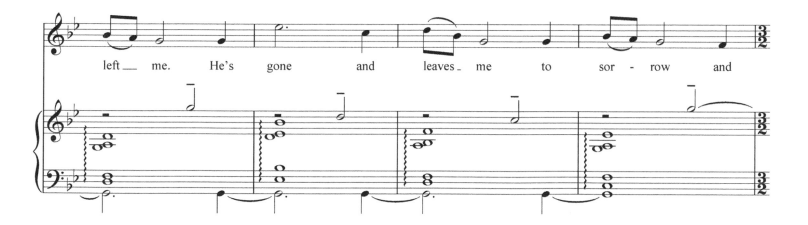

left __ me. He's gone and leaves __ me to sor - row and

moan. __

sor - row and moan. He's gone, _____

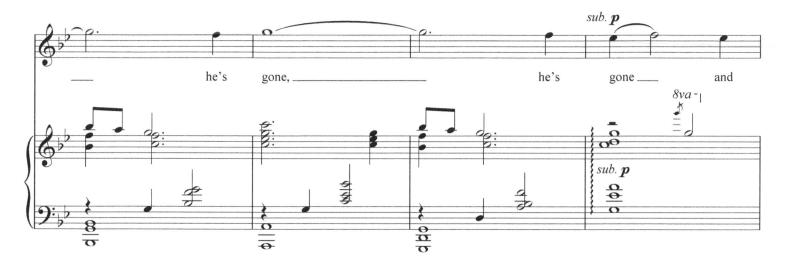

_____ he's gone, _____ he's gone _____ and

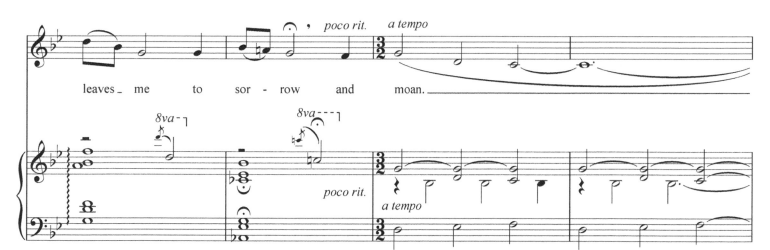

leaves _ me to sor - row and moan. _____

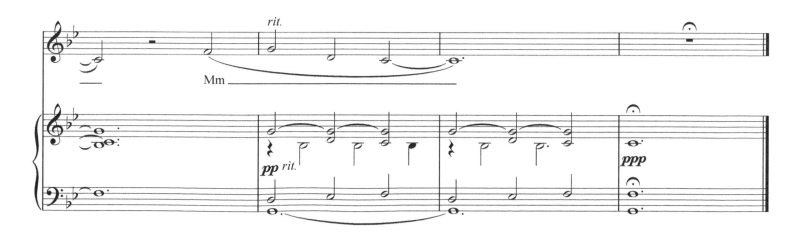

Mm _____

I Gave My Love a Cherry
(The Riddle Song)

Folksong from the Kentucky Mountains
arranged by Richard Walters

end. I gave my love a ba-by with no cry - in'.

2. How can there be a

cher-ry that has no stone? How can there be a chick-en that

has no bone? How can there be a sto-ry that has no

end? How can there be a ba - by with no cry - in'?

(pp)
(p)
3. A cher - ry when it's

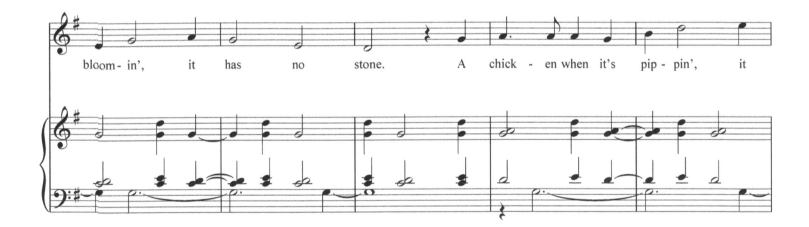

bloom - in', it has no stone. A chick - en when it's pip - pin', it

cresc. *espr.*
poco cresc. *più esp.*
has no bone. The sto - ry that I love you, it

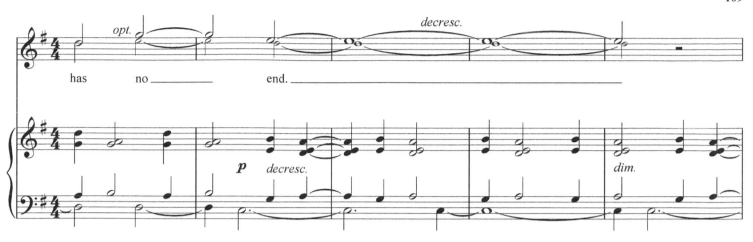

has   no _____   end. _____

A   ba - by when it's sleep - in'   makes   no ____

cry -   in'. _____

Johnny Has Gone for a Soldier

American Revolutionary War Song
arranged by Richard Walters

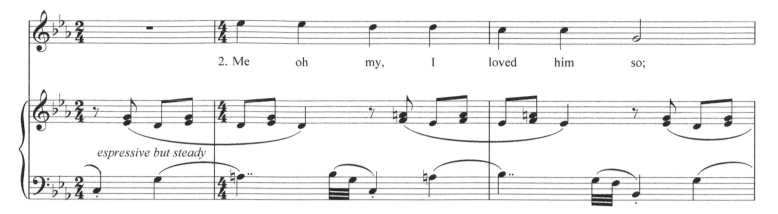

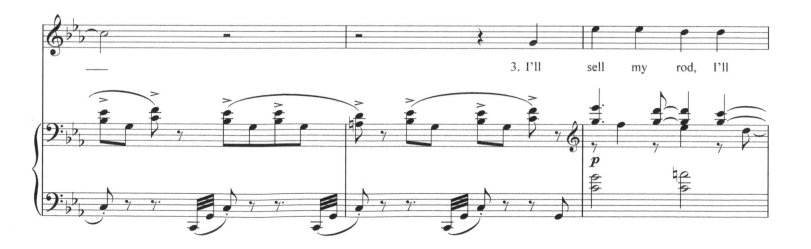

sell my reel, like-wise I'll sell my spin-nin' wheel and

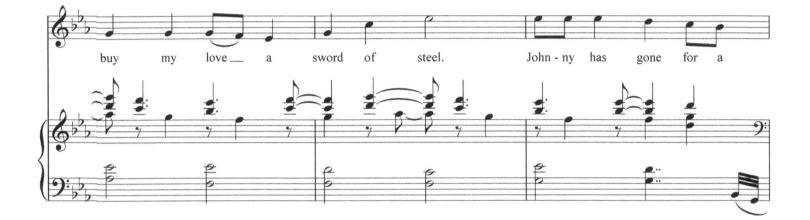

buy my love ___ a sword of steel. John-ny has gone for a

sol - dier. _____

Largo
(p)

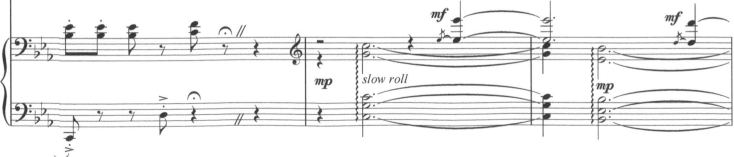

4. I'll dye my dress, I'll ___ dye it red

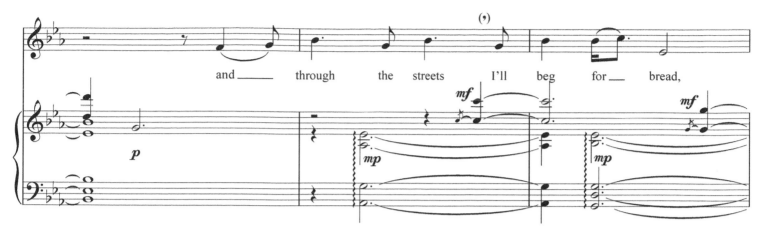

and _____ through the streets I'll beg for _____ bread,

for the lad I love _____ from me has fled. _____

Tempo I

John-ny has gone, John-ny

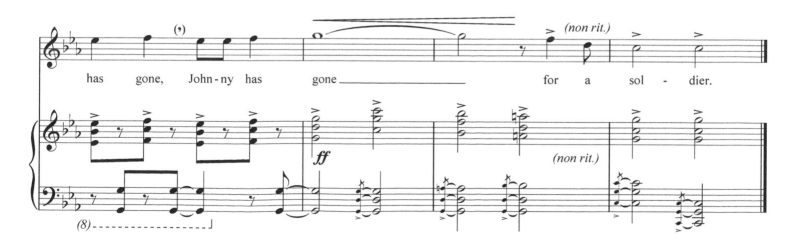

has gone, John-ny has gone _____ for a sol - dier.

for Robert

Let Us Break Bread Together

African–American Spiritual
arranged by Richard Walters

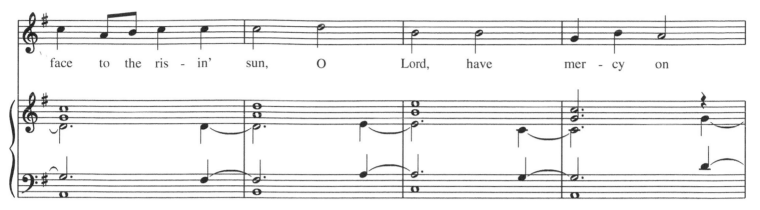

face to the ris - in' sun, O Lord, have mer - cy on

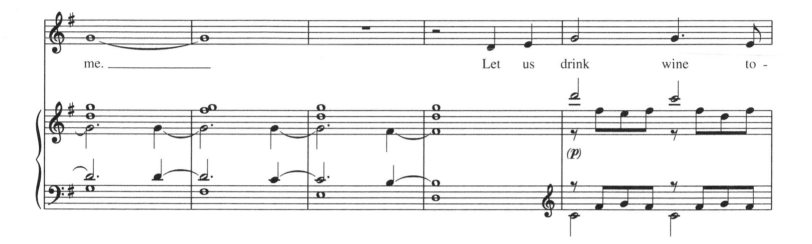

me. _____ Let us drink wine to -

geth-er on our knees, _____ Let us drink wine to -

geth-er on our knees. _____ When I fall on my

cresc. poco

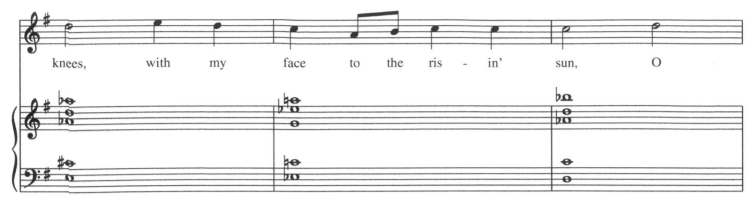

knees,   with   my   face   to   the   ris - in'   sun,   O

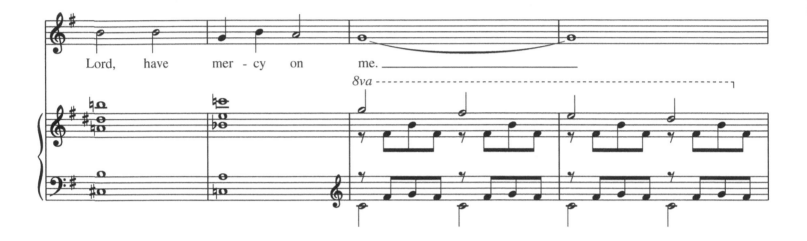

Lord,   have   mer - cy   on   me.

8va

Let   us   praise   God   to -

mf

geth - er   on   our   knees,   Let   us   praise   God   to -

(either R.H. or L.H.)

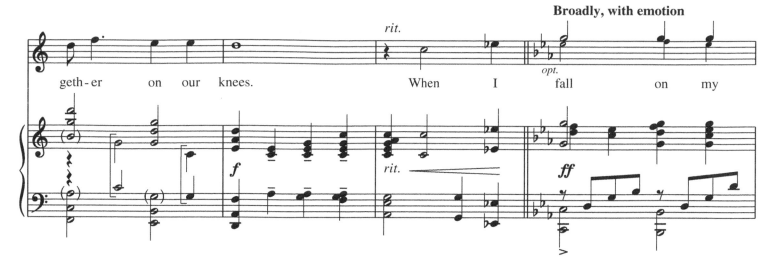

geth- er   on   our   knees.   When   I   fall   on   my

knees,   with   my   face   to   the   ris - in'   sun, _____

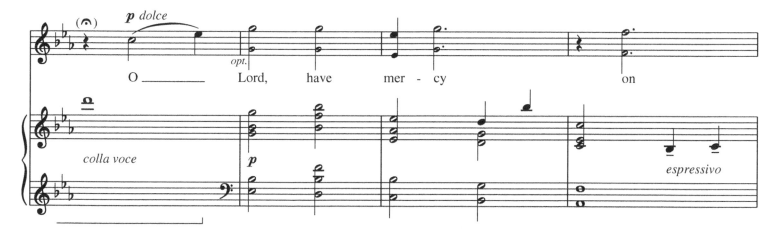

O _____   Lord,   have   mer - cy   on

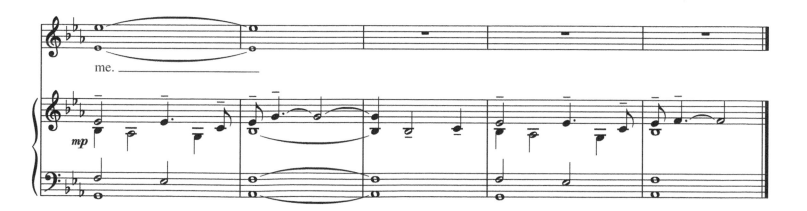

me. _____

Mighty Day

American Folksong
Commemorating the great Galveston flood of 1900
arranged by Bryan Stanley

Might-y day! _____ Might-y day! _____ 1. I re-mem-ber one Sep-tem-ber when the storm winds swept the town. Wom-en and chil-dren were dy'-in, Lord, _____ and _____ death, _____ and

death _____ was___ all___ a - round!

Allegro ♩ = 74

2. There was a sea - wall guard - ing Gal - ves - ton to

keep the wa - ters down, but the high tide from the o - cean, Lord,__ put__

wa - ter in the town. Was - n't it a might - y day? _____

Was-n't it a might - y day?_____ Was-n't it a might - y day, Great

God, that morn-ing when the storm winds swept the town! Was-n't it a

might - y day?_____ Was-n't it a might - y day?_____ Was-n't it a might - y day, Great

God, that morn-ing when the storm winds swept the town! Ah_____

3. Well, the

trum - pets gave them warn - ing: "You'd bet - ter leave this

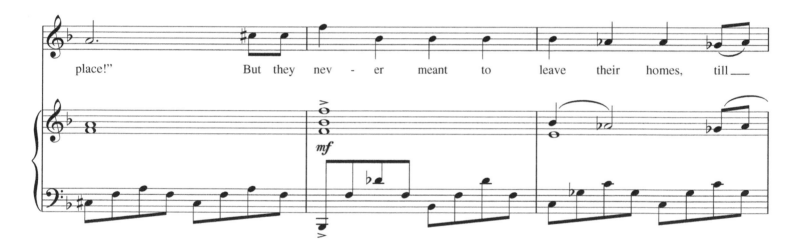

place!" But they nev - er meant to leave their homes, till death was in their

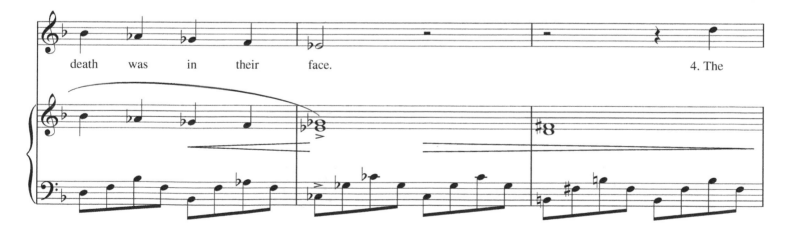

death was in their face. 4. The

trains, they all were load - ed with peo - ple leav - ing town; the

tracks gave way to the o - cean, Lord, __ and the trains went fall - ing down. A

might - y day? _____ Was-n't it a might - y day? _____ 5. The

wa - ters, like some riv - er, came a rush - ing to and fro. I saw my fath - er

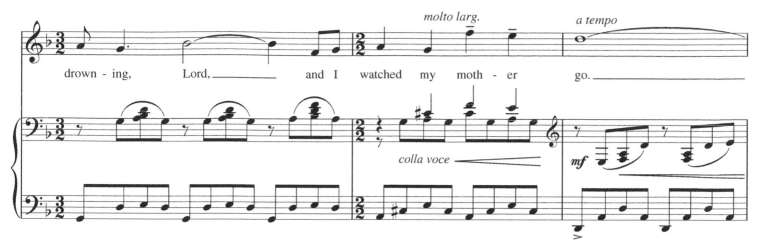

drown-ing, Lord,_____ and I watched my moth-er go._____

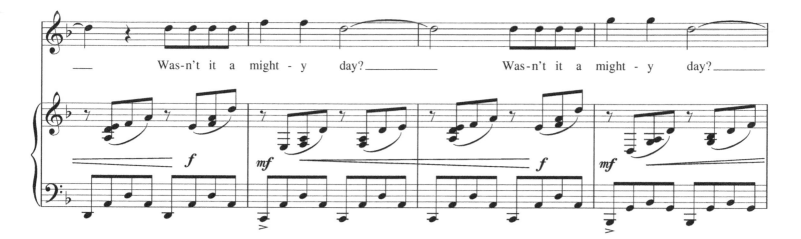

___ Was-n't it a might-y day?_____ Was-n't it a might-y day?_____

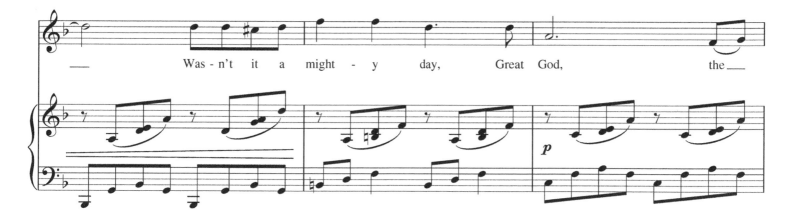

___ Was-n't it a might-y day, Great God, the ___

storm winds swept___ through the town! Was-n't it a

124

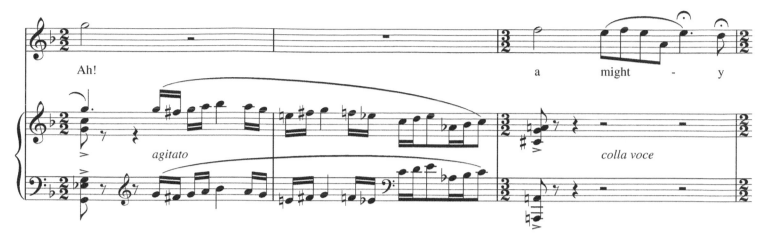

Ah!   a might-y

Tempo I

day!   It was a might-y day,_____   it was a

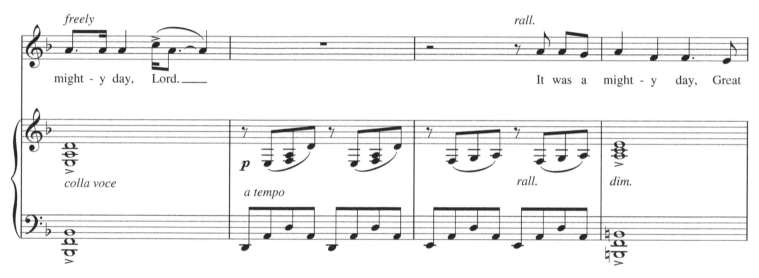

might-y day, Lord.____   It was a might-y day, Great

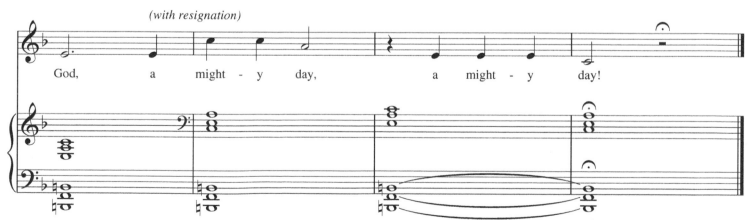

God,   a might-y   day,   a   might-y   day!

Nine Hundred Miles

American Blues Folksong
arranged by Richard Walters

* pronounced "tuh" ("u" as in "put")

home to-mor-row night,___ 'cause I'm nine hun-dred miles from_ my

home. _____ And I hate t' hear that lone-some whis - tle

p

blow, _____ that long, lone - some train___ whis - tle

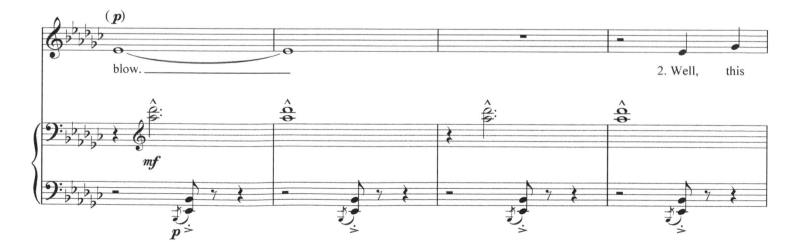

(*p*)

blow. _____ 2. Well, this

mf

p

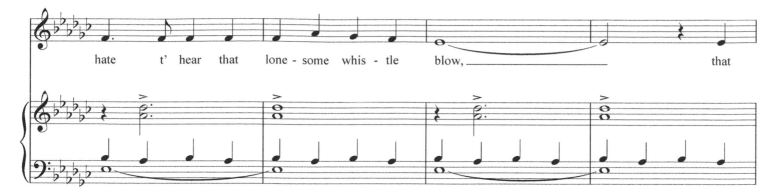

hate t' hear that lone-some whis-tle blow, _____ that

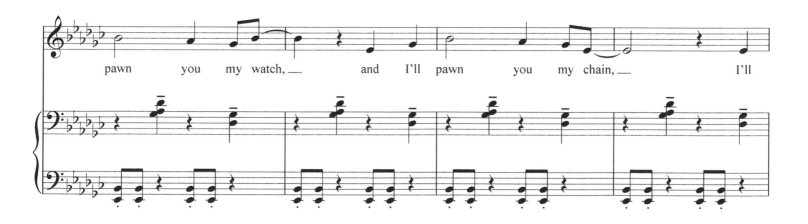

long, lone-some train __ whis-tle blow. 3. Well, I'll

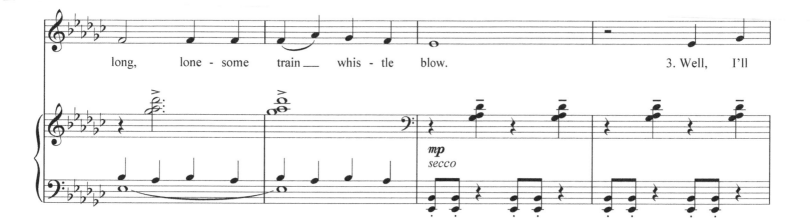

pawn you my watch, __ and I'll pawn you my chain, __ I'll

pawn you my gold-en dia-mond ring. And if this

train runs me right, ___ I'll be home to-mor-row night, ___ 'cause I'm

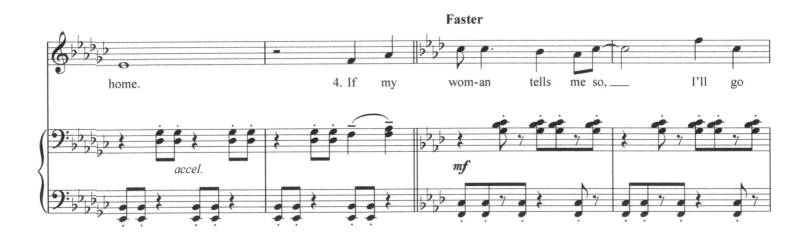

nine hun - dred, nine hun - dred, nine hun - dred miles from _ my

Faster

home.   4. If my wom-an tells me so, ___ I'll go

rail - road - in' no more, ___ I'll side - track that wheel - er and go

home. _____ *opt.* And if this train runs me right, ___ I'll be

home by Sat - ur - day night, ___ 'cause I'm nine _____

decresc. *mp* *p*

___ hun - dred miles _____ I'm nine _____

crescendo *poco* *a* *poco*

___ hun - dred miles, _____ I'm *opt.* nine _____

ff

hun - dred miles from my home. _____

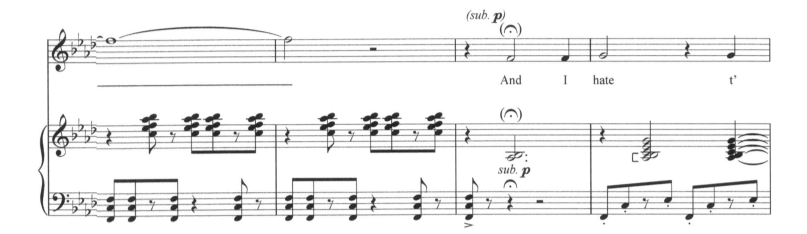

_____ (sub. **p**)

And I hate t'

hear that lone - some whis - tle blow, _____

that long, _____

sim.

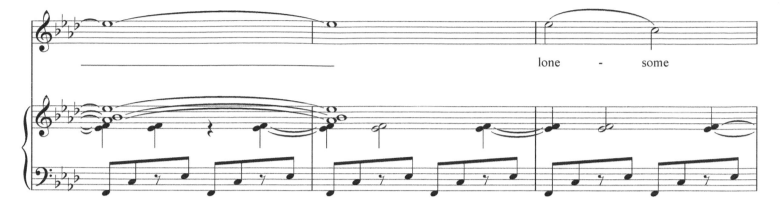

lone - some whis - tle blow.

The River in the Pines

19th Century Midwestern American
arranged by Bryan Stanley

1. O Mar - y was a mai - den when the birds be - gan to sing. She was fair - er than the bloom - ing rose so ear - ly in the

spring. 2. Her thoughts were gay and

hap - py ___ and the morn - ing gay and fine, for her lov - er was a

lum - ber boy from the riv - er in the pines. ___

3. Now

A little slower ♩. = 52

Char - lie, he got mar - ried _____ to his

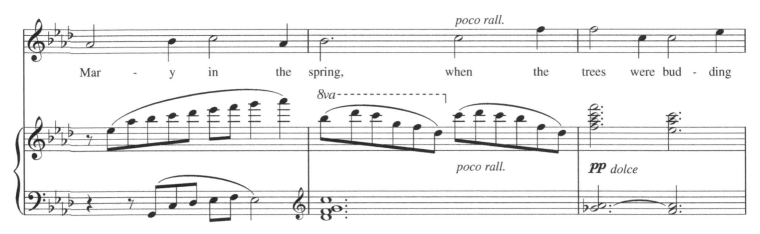

Mar - y in the spring, when the trees were bud - ding

poco rall.

pp dolce

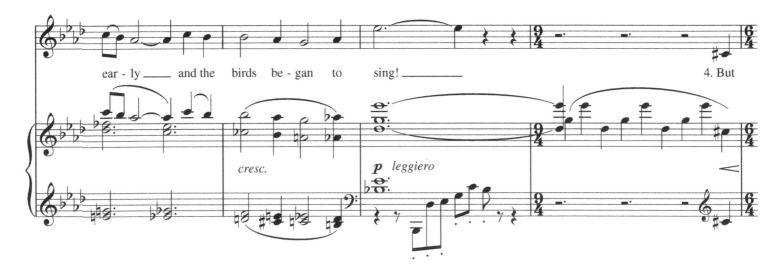

ear - ly _____ and the birds be - gan to sing! _____ 4. But

cresc.

p leggiero

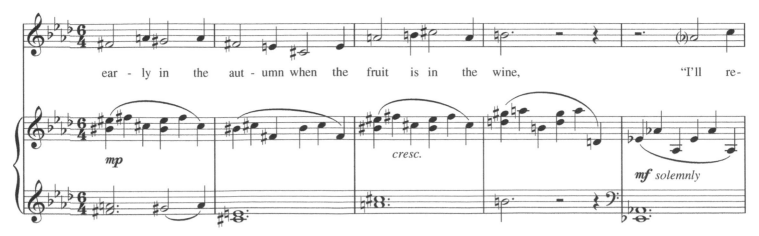

ear - ly in the au - tumn when the fruit is in the wine, "I'll re-

mp

cresc.

mf solemnly

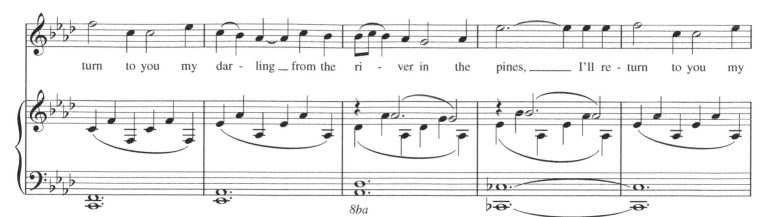

turn to you my dar - ling __ from the ri - ver in the pines, ___ I'll re - turn to you my

8ba

More broadly

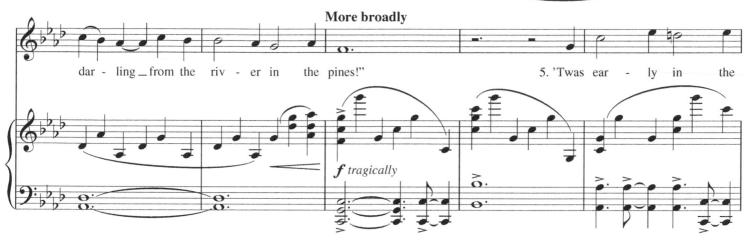

dar - ling __ from the riv - er in the pines!" 5. 'Twas ear - ly in the

f tragically

mor - ning in Wis - con - sin's drear - y clime, when he rode the sav - age rap - ids for the

last and fa - tal time. ___ 6. They found his bod - y

dim.

pp *eerily, with mist*

138

ly - ing on the rock - y shore be - low where the si - lent wat - er

rip - ples and the whis' - pring ce - dars blow. 6. Now

ev - 'ry raft of lum - ber that comes from the Chip - pe -

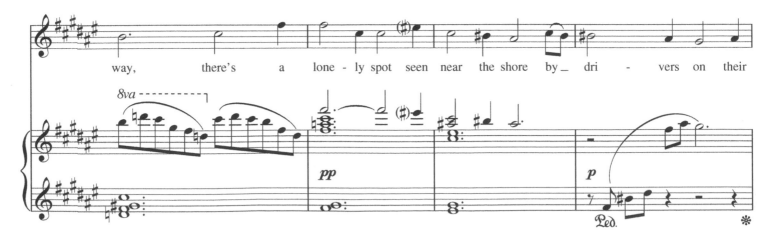

way, there's a lone - ly spot seen near the shore by _ dri - vers on their

Tempo primo

way.   7. They

plant wild flow'rs u - pon it in the mor - ning gay and

fine.   'Tis _____ the   grave _____ of two young

lov - ers from the riv - er in _____ the pines!

Sacramento

American Sea Chanty
arranged by Bryan Stanley

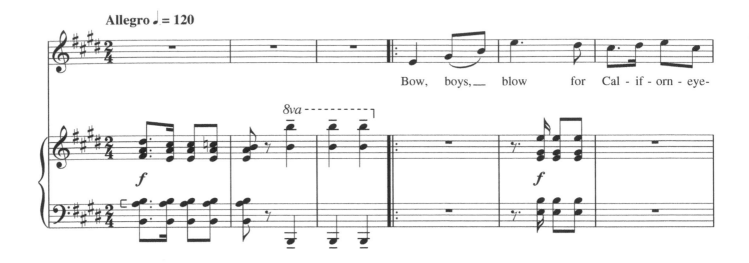

Bow, boys,___ blow for Cal - if - orn - eye-

o! There's plen - ty o' gold so I've been told, on the banks of the Sac - ra - men - to, on the

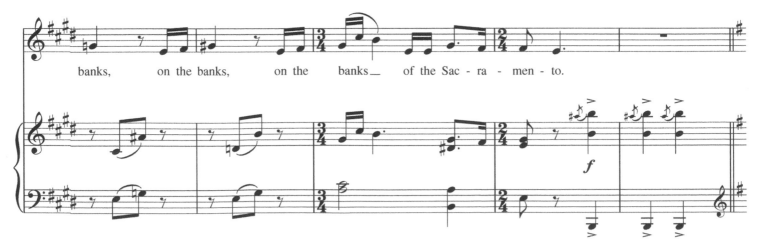

banks, on the banks, on the banks___ of the Sac - ra - men - to.

1. Oh, a - round Cape Horn we are bound for to go. Too - mee
2. Oh, a - round Cape Horn in the month of May, Too - mee

hoo - dah! Too - mee hoo - dah! A - round Cape Horn through the sleet an' the snow. Too - mee
hoo - dah! Too - mee hoo - dah! A - round Cape Horn is a ver - y long way. Too - mee

hoo - dah, hoo - dah day! hoo - dah, hoo - dah day! A -
hoo - dah, hoo - dah day! hoo - dah, hoo - dah, day! A -

round Cape Horn through the sleet an' the snow. Too - mee hoo - dah, hoo - dah
round Cape Horn is a ver - y long way, Too - mee hoo - dah, hoo - dah

cresc.

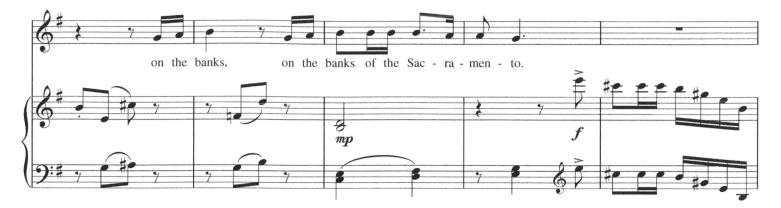

on the banks, on the banks of the Sac - ra - men - to.

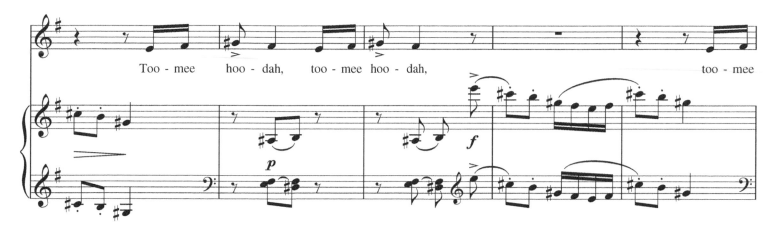

Too - mee hoo - dah, too - mee hoo - dah, too - mee

hoo - dah, hoo - dah day! Too - mee hoo! Too - mee hoo! Too - mee hoo - dah, hoo - dah

day! _____

Sail Around

19th Century American Folksong of the Plains
arranged by Richard Walters

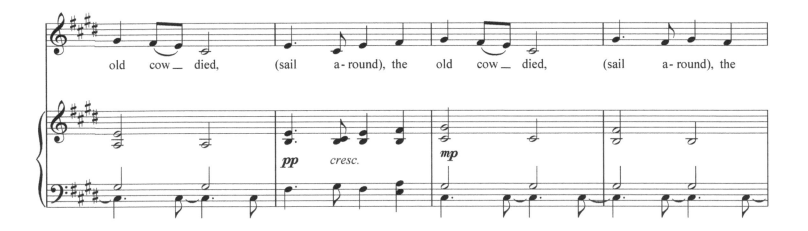

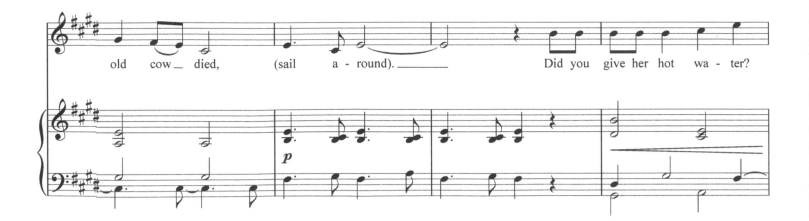

146

what the world ailed her? Did she die of the chol-er-a? Yes,_____ ma'am_____

The old cow_ died, (sail a-round), the old cow_ died,

(sail a - round). _____ Did the buz-zards,they come?_ Yes, ma'am. Did the

buz - zards, they eat her? Yes, ma'am And did

Shenandoah

19th Century American Chanty
arranged by Richard Walters

wide Mis - sou - ri.*   2. Oh,

Shen - an - do', _____ I love your daugh - ter, a -

way _____ your roll - in' riv - er.   For

her I'd cross _____ your roam - in' wa - ter.   A -

* Missouruh

way, _____ I'm bound a - way 'cross the

wide Mis - sou - ri.

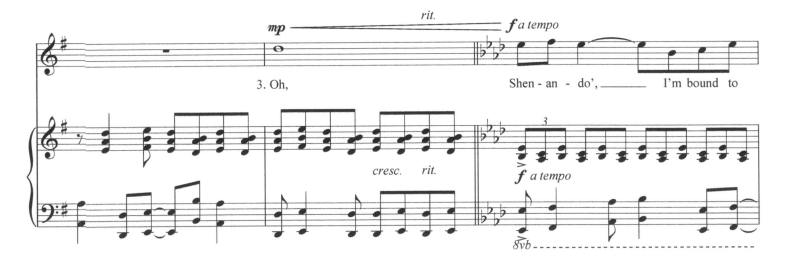

3. Oh, Shen - an - do', _____ I'm bound to

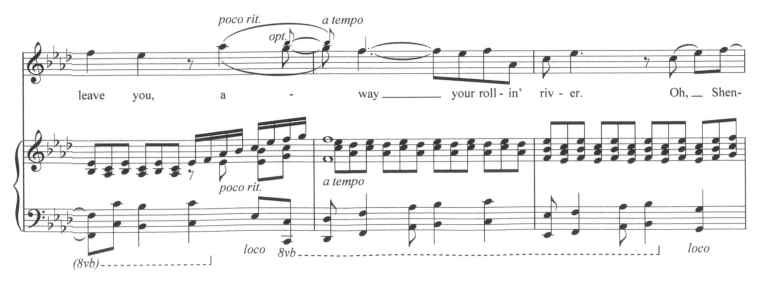

leave you, a - way _____ your roll - in' riv - er. Oh, __ Shen-

Shen - an - do - ah, _____ Shen - an - do - ah. _____

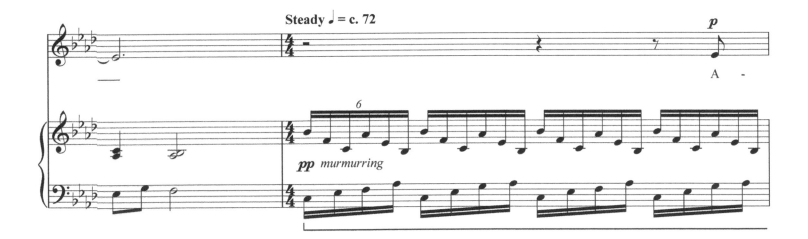

Steady ♩ = c. 72

A -

way, I'm bound a -

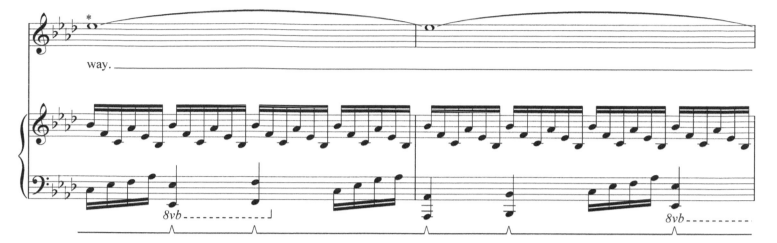

way.

rit.

ppp

* Hold this note softly as long as you can and gracefully release as necessary.

This page has been left blank to facilitate page turns.

Wayfaring Stranger

Southern American Folksong
arranged by Richard Walters

This song seems like a spiritual, and it may well be one, but those origins have been unconfirmed.

roam. I'm on-ly go - in' o-ver Jor-dan, I'm on-ly

go - in' o-ver home.

2. I know dark clouds_____ will gath-er 'round me. I know my

way_____ is rough and steep, but gol-den fields_____ lie out be-

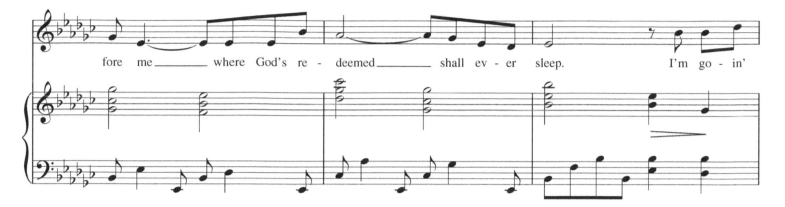

fore me _____ where God's re - deemed _____ shall ev - er sleep. I'm go - in'

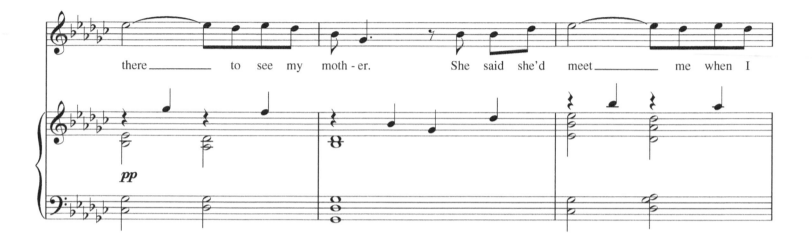

there _____ to see my moth - er. She said she'd meet _____ me when I

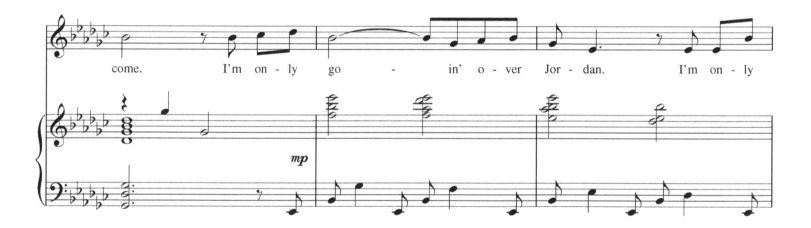

come. I'm on - ly go - in' o - ver Jor - dan. I'm on - ly

go - in' o - ver home.

3. I'll soon be free_____ from ev - ry tri - al, my bod - y

sleep_____ in the church - yard. I'll drop the cross_____ of self de -

ni - al and en - ter on_____ my great re - ward.

I'm go - in' there_____ to see my Sa - vior, to sing his

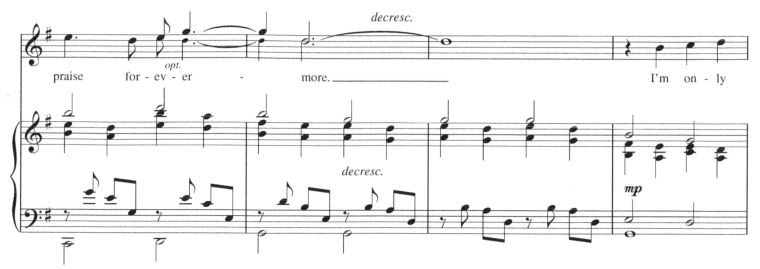

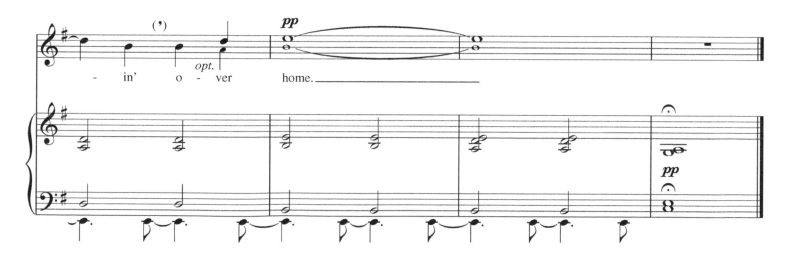

Single Girl

19th Century American Folksong
arranged by Richard Walters

1. When I was sing-le, go

dressed neat and fine, now I am mar-ried, go rag-ged all the time. I

wish I were a sing-le girl a-gain, Lord, Lord, oh, I wish I were a sing-le girl a-gain.

2. When ___ I was sing-le, my shoes they did squeak,

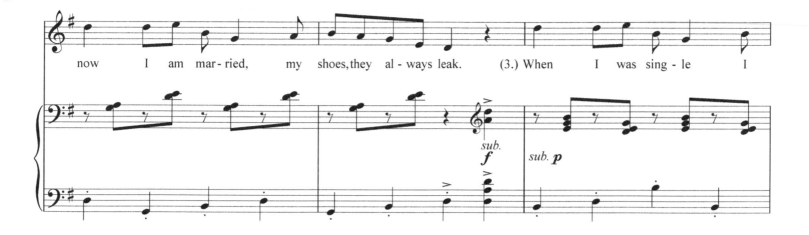

now I am mar-ried, my shoes, they al-ways leak. (3.) When I was sing-le I

ate bis-cuit pie, now I am mar-ried, eat corn-bread or die. I

wish I were a sing-le girl a-gain, Lord, Lord, oh I wish I were a sing-le girl a-

gain.   4. Two ___ lit-tle ba-bies all for to re-tain,

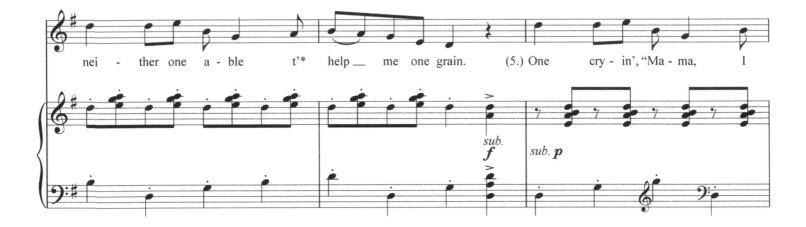

nei - ther one a - ble t'* help ___ me one grain.   (5.) One   cry - in', "Ma - ma,   I

wan - na piece o' bread."   One   cry - in', "Ma - ma, I don' wan - na go t' bed.   I

wish I were a sing - le girl a - gain, Lord, Lord, Oh I wish I were a sing - le girl a-

* pronounced "tuh" ("u" as in "put")

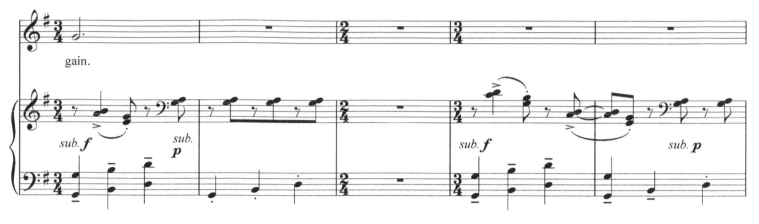

gain.

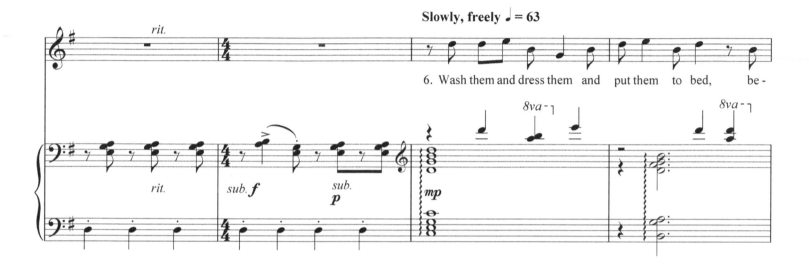

Slowly, freely ♩ = 63

6. Wash them and dress them and put them to bed, be -

fore that drunk man curs - es us and wish - es we were dead. I

Andante ♩ = 80

wish I were a sing - le girl a - gain, Lord, Lord, oh I wish I were a sing - le girl a - gain.

Soldier, Soldier, Will You Marry Me

Colonial American Folksong
arranged by Richard Walters

This melody is probably of English origin; the American adaptation dates from c. 1700.

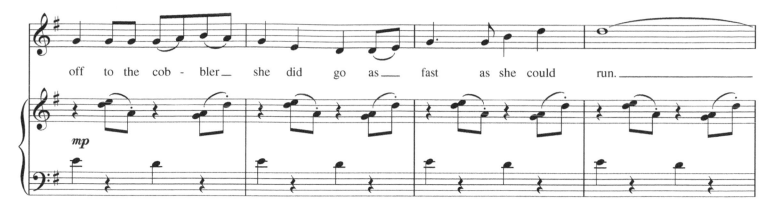

off to the cob - bler___ she did go as___ fast as she could run._____

___ She brought him back the fin - est that was there and the

sol - dier put them___ on._____

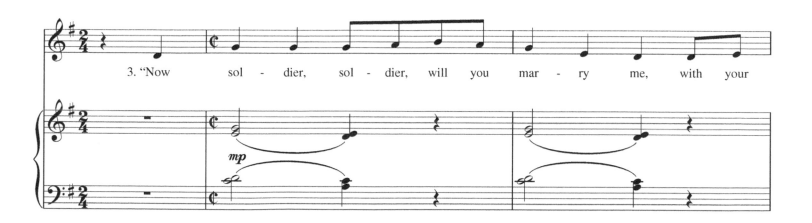

3. "Now sol - dier, sol - dier, will you mar - ry me, with your

166

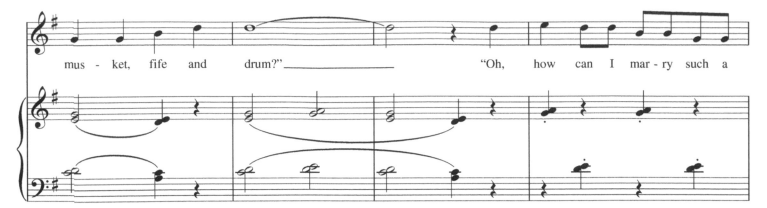

mus - ket, fife and drum?" "Oh, how can I mar - ry such a

pret - ty lit - tle girl when I have no coat to put on?"

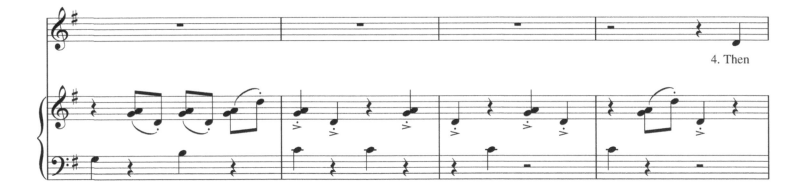

4. Then

off to the tai - lor she did go as fast as she could run.

she brought him back the fin - est that was there and the sol - dier put it

on.

Meno mosso *dolce* *opt.*

5. "Now,___ sol - dier, sol - dier, will you mar - ry

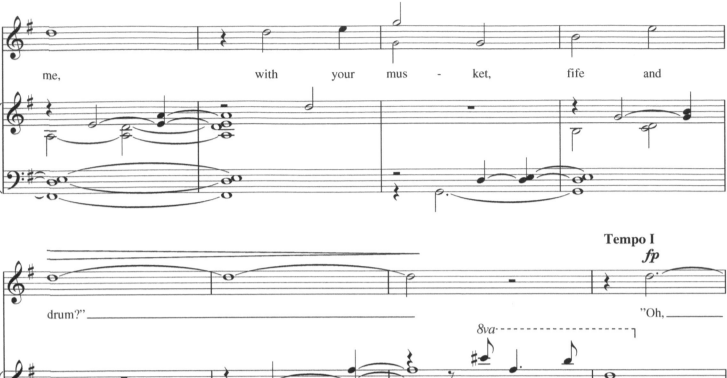

me, with your mus - ket, fife and

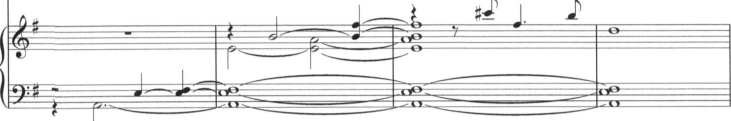

drum?" "Oh,

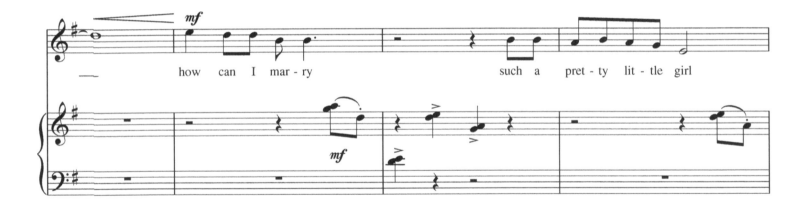

how can I mar - ry such a pret - ty lit - tle girl

with a wife and ba - by at home?"

for Carol and Anne

We Are Climbing Jacob's Ladder

(duet)

African-American Spiritual
Arranged by Richard Walters

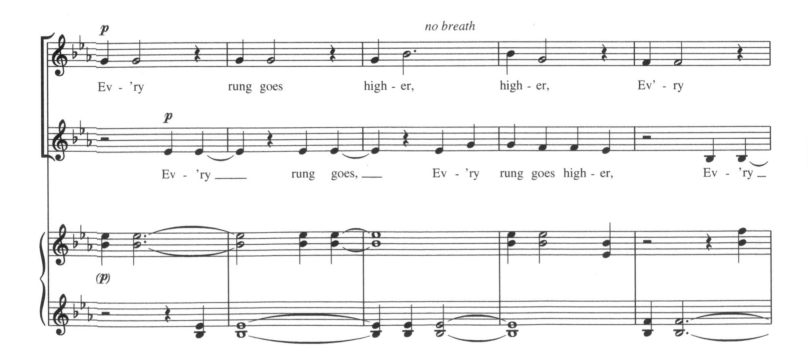

174

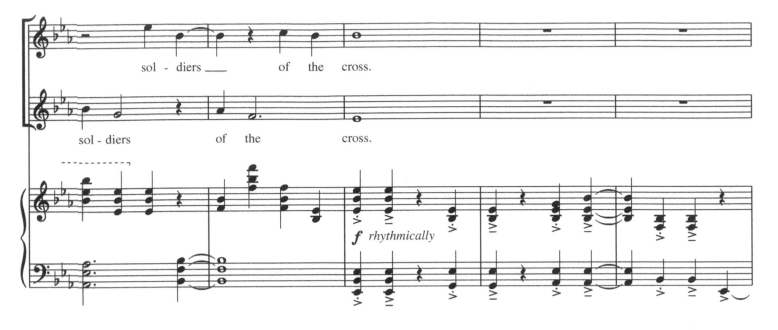

sol - diers ___ of the cross.

sol - diers of the cross.

More Broadly

Keep on ___ climb - ing, ___ we will sure - ly make it, ___

Keep on climb - ing, we will make it,

A Little Slower

We are climb-ing Ja-cob's lad-der, We are

We are climb-ing Ja-cob's gol-den lad-der We are

We Are Climbing Jacob's Ladder

(Solo Version)

African-American Spiritual
arranged by Richard Walters

Moderately, very steady ♩ = 66

1. We are climb-ing Ja-cob's lad-der we are climb-ing Ja-cob's lad-der, we are climb-ing Ja-cob's lad-der, sol-diers of the cross.

2. Ev - 'ry

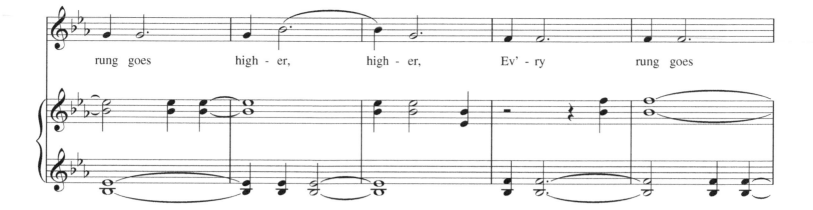

rung goes high - er, high - er, Ev' - ry rung goes

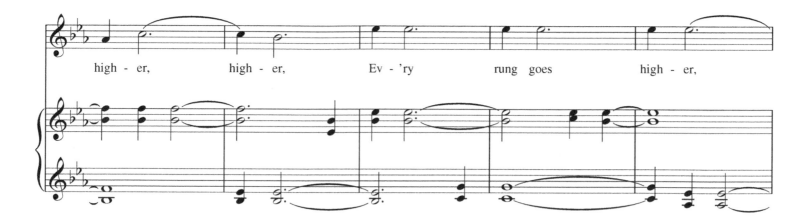

high - er, high - er, Ev - 'ry rung goes high - er,

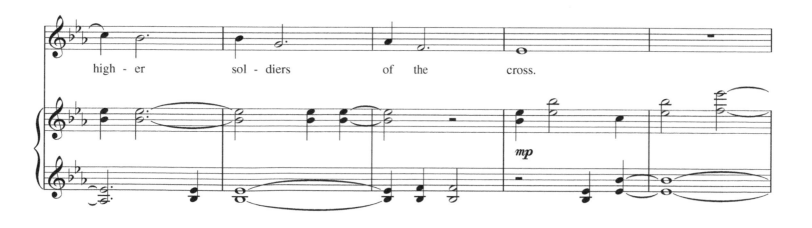

high - er sol - diers of the cross.

180

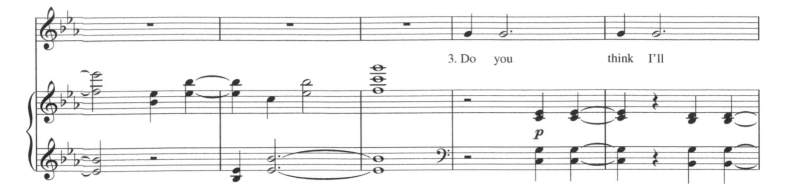

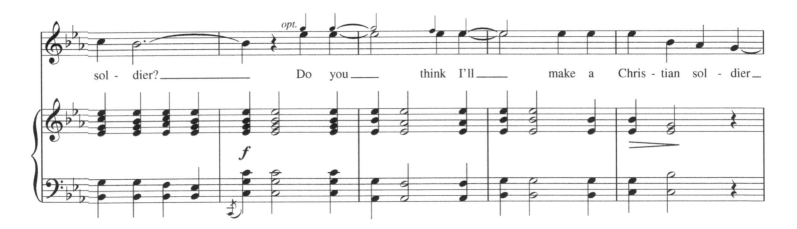

More Broadly ♩ = 84

5. Keep on climb - ing, we will make it,

keep on climb - ing, we will make it, keep on

climb - ing, we will make it, sol - diers of the

Tempo primo ♩ = 66

cross.

a tempo

We are climb-ing

Ja-cob's lad-der, we are climb-ing Ja-cob's lad-der,

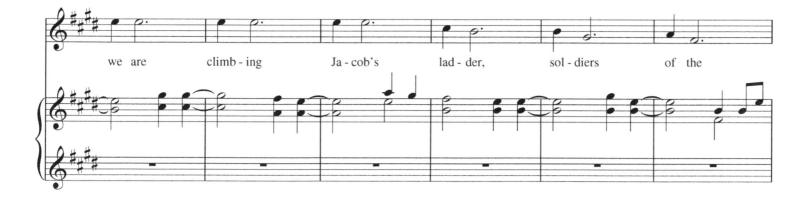

we are climb-ing Ja-cob's lad-der, sol-diers of the

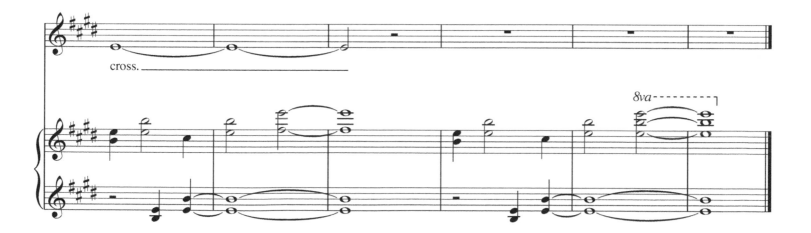

cross.

8va----------

The Streets of Laredo

19th Century American Cowboy Song
based on the Irish Ballad "A Handful of Laurel"
arranged by Richard Walters

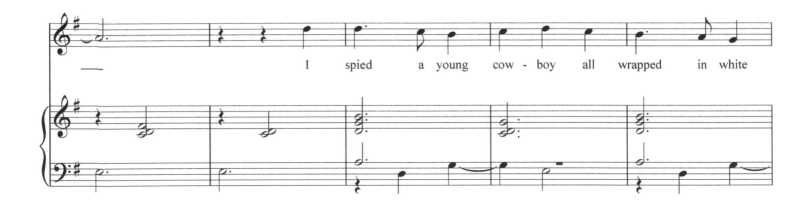

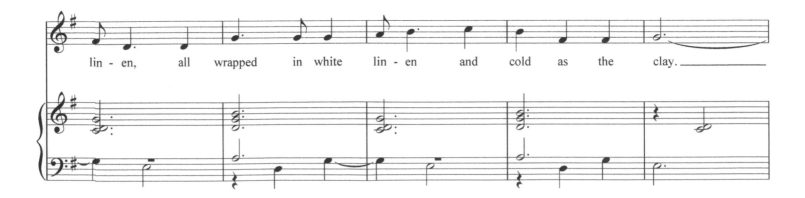

Spoken: *And he said,* 2. "I see by your out-fit that

you are a cow-boy." These words he did say as I bold-ly walked

by. _____ "Come sit down be-side me and

hear my sad sto-ry. I'm shot in the chest and I know I must

die._____

3. It was once in the sad-dle I

warmly R.H. cantabile

used to go dash-in', once in the sad-dle I used to ride a-

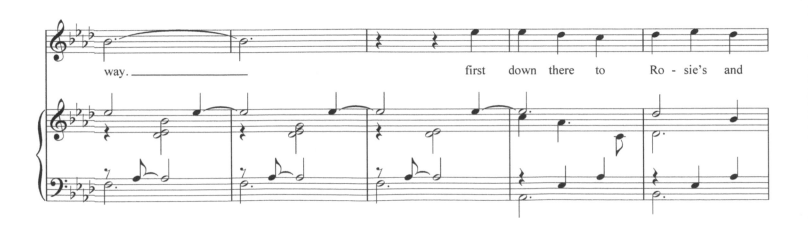

way._____ first down there to Ro-sie's and

then to the card-house. Got shot in the chest and I'm dy-in' to-

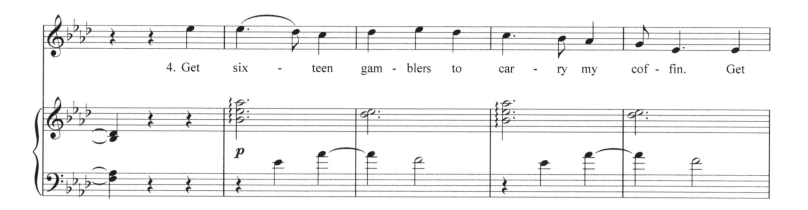

day.

4. Get six-teen gam-blers to car-ry my cof-fin. Get

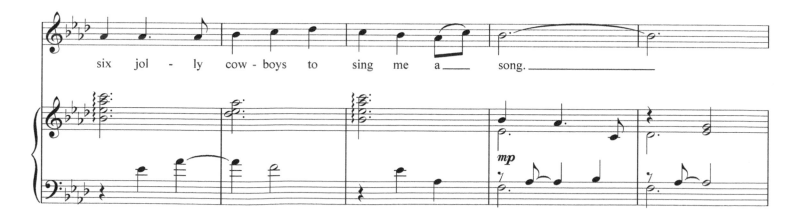

six jol-ly cow-boys to sing me a song.

Take me to the grave - yard and lay the sod o'er me, for

I'm a young cow - boy and I know I've done wrong.

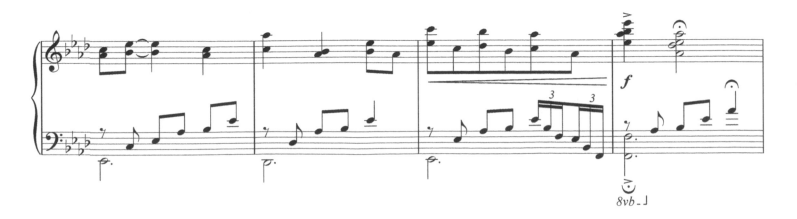

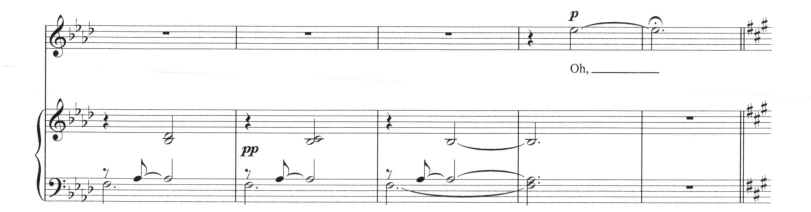

Oh, _____

Slowly ♩ = 63

(throughout this verse he becomes increasingly "sleepy" with death)

bang   the   drum   slow - ly _____   and

play   the   fife   low - ly, _____

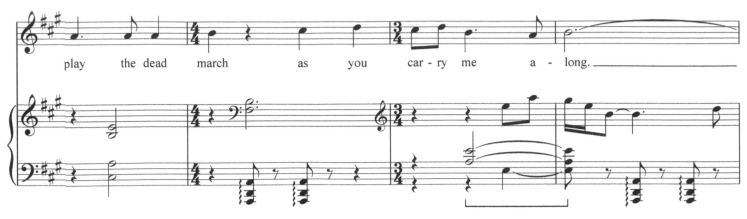

play the dead march as you car - ry me a - long._____

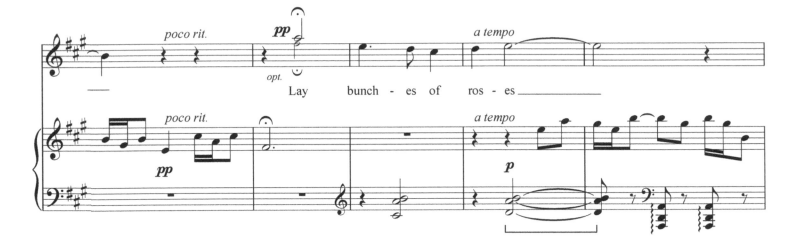

_____ Lay bunch - es of ros - es _____

all o - ver my cof - fin, ___ ros - es to

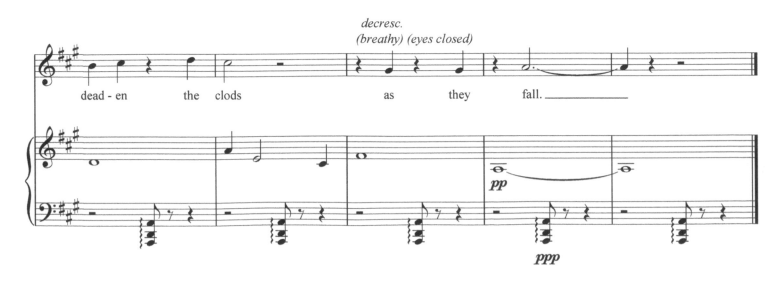

dead - en the clods as they fall._____

Whistle, Daughter, Whistle

American Folksong
arranged by Bryan Stanley

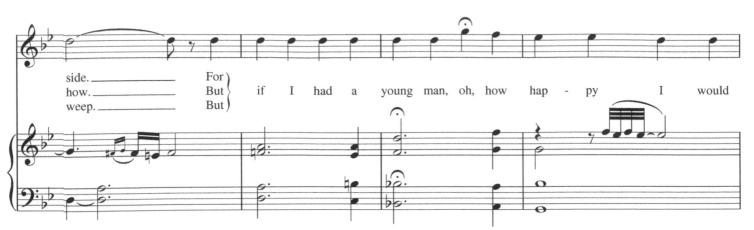

side._____ For
how._____ But } if I had a young man, oh, how hap - py I would
weep._____ But

be, for I am tired and wear-y of my sin-gu-lar-i -

ty.   ty.

ty.

mf

4. "Whis - tle, daugh - ter, whis - tle, and you shall have a man." I

can - not whis - tle, moth - er... *Whistle*

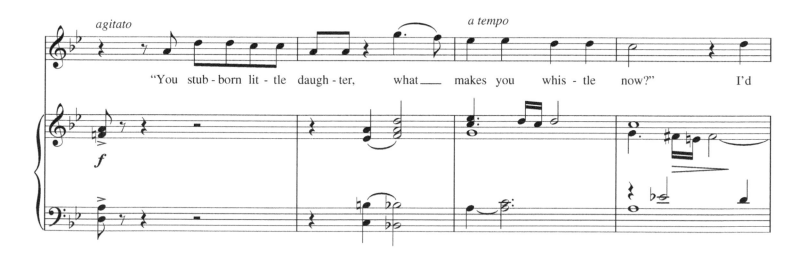

"You stub - born lit - tle daugh - ter, what__ makes you whis - tle now?" I'd

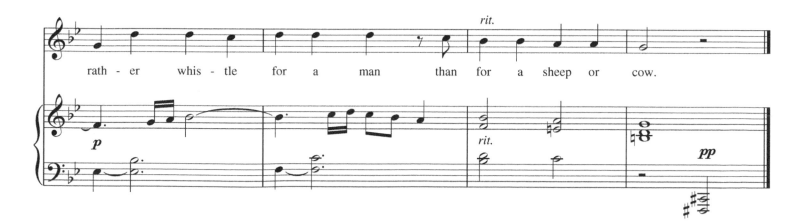

rath - er whis - tle for a man than for a sheep or cow.

for Paul and Lou

Wondrous Love
(duet)

American Folk Hymn
arranged by Richard Walters

bliss   To   bear   the   dread - ful   curse   for   my

soul,   for   my   soul,   To   bear   the   dread - ful   curse   for   my

soul.

mp

lay a - side His crown for my soul, for my soul, He

soul, _____ O my

lay a - side His crown for my soul.

soul. _____

High Voice:

What

won - drous love is this, O my soul, O my

Medium Voice:

What won - drous love is

soul, What won - drous love is this, O my

this, O my soul O my soul, What

Wondrous Love

(solo version)

American Folk Hymn
arranged by Richard Walters

Slow, steady (♩ = 76)

What won-drous love is this, O my soul, O my soul, What won-drous love is this. O my soul. What won-drous love is this that caused the Lord of

bliss   To   bear   the   dread - ful   curse   for   my

soul,   for   my   soul,   To   bear   the   dread - ful   curse   for   my

soul.

mp

203

soul,   What won - drous love is this that ____

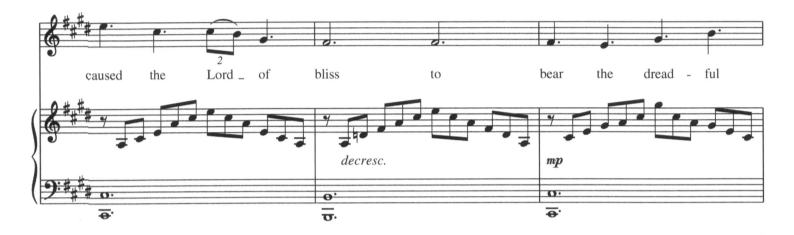

caused the Lord _ of bliss to bear the dread - ful

curse for my soul, for my soul, to

bear the dread - ful curse for my soul, _____

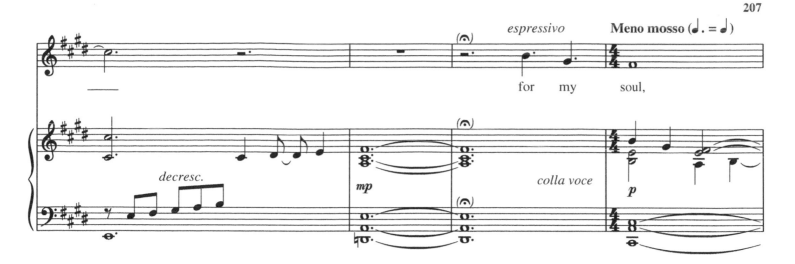